IMMORTALITY
FUNERARY RITES & CUSTOMS

D1147401

IMMORTALITY
FUNERARY RITES & CUSTOMS

C. E. VULLIAMY

SENATE

Immortality

First published in 1926 as *Immortal Man* by
Methuen and Company Ltd, London

This edition first published in 1997 by Senate,
an imprint of Random House UK Ltd,
Random House, 20 Vauxhall Bridge Road,
London SW1V 2SA

Copyright © C. E. Vulliamy 1926

All rights reserved. No part of this publication may be
reproduced, stored in a retrieval system or transmitted,
in any form or by any means, electronic, mechanical,
photocopying, recording or otherwise, without the prior
permission of the copyright owners.

ISBN 1 85958 487 X

Printed and bound in Guernsey by
The Guernsey Press Co Ltd

PREFACE

THE subject of this book is the belief in the immortality of man. It has been my intention to trace that belief in the evidence afforded by prehistoric burials, and to describe its manifestation among primitive races. I have sought to discover in what way we are influenced, at the present time, by primitive custom, and to examine our attitude towards the problem of survival. But I have no wish to present any theory of my own, and if particular views seem to have been given undue prominence, that must be set down to the unconscious bias from which no writer is ever free.

Where I am specially indebted to any one author, or where it has seemed necessary to state the source of my information, I have incorporated acknowledgment or reference in the text.

The bibliography contains the titles of all the important works which I have consulted. In common with every student of primitive man, I owe much to the writings of Spencer and Gillen, Howitt, Rivers, Sir J. G. Frazer, and A. R. Brown. For translations of Egyptian texts, and for information on many points relating to the beliefs of ancient Egypt, I am indebted to the works of Sir Wallis Budge.

C. E. V.

April, 1926.

CONTENTS

IMMORTAL MAN

CHAPTER I

IMMORTALITY

The origin of the belief in immortality—The nature of the soul, according to primitive man—Eschatology : the fate of the soul—Relation between the dead and the living—Death-dealers.

THE ORIGIN OF THE BELIEF IN IMMORTALITY

THE Catholic honouring a holy bone, and the Polynesian consulting the painted skull of his ancestor, are both of them united by a belief which (if the evidence is correctly interpreted) would appear to be coeval with humanity itself ; the belief in the immortality of the soul. It is a belief which comes into existence long before man reaches the stage at which he is capable of forming definitely religious and moral ideas. In some form or other, it is practically universal. We must therefore expect to find its beginnings in some common experience of primitive mankind.

The evidence which we are about to examine will show us that, in his most ancient or most primitive state, man has believed, and believes, that the consciousness of the individual is not extinguished by bodily death. With occasional reservations and exceptions, the primitive mind regards the ghostly life as a reality beyond the reach of question or dispute ; and although the idea of that life ranges from the most dismal and horrible fantasies to the most sublime imaginations, the fundamental thought is always the same : the body dies, but not the spirit. From whence arises this tremendous conviction ?

The shadow, the reflected image, and the breath of man, things intangible yet personal, may be reckoned among the possible objective suggestions of immortality. In some cases, the name for the soul of a dead person may also be used to denote the shadow of a living person (or, indeed, as with the Cheyenne Indians, the shadow of any living thing), and the supposed connection between the breath and the soul is well known. To these suggestions may be added things imperfectly seen in the deep gloom of forest or jungle, in twilight or moonlight, inexplicable noises, the mere aspect or the accidental movement of a corpse. But for the most probable origin we must turn to the question of subjective or inward vision, to an experience common to all men in all ages, to dreams. In dream and hallucination man perceives, or thinks he perceives, things of which he is not made aware by his ordinary senses. The belief that the dead appear in dreams and in visions of the night is not only world-wide but is strongly in evidence among civilised peoples ; and in dealing with the sources of the belief in immortality we shall do well to give something more than a casual attention to the subject of dreams.

A very primitive or simple person, or a very young child, is not able to distinguish clearly between the experience of the dreaming mind and the experience of the wide-awake consciousness. For them, a dream has a character of " reality " which sets it on a level with any ordinary occurrence. Now, be the reason what it may (and there is no difficulty in finding a psychological explanation), there is in all people a very marked tendency to dream of the dead. A primitive man who has dreamed of a dead person believes that he has actually seen the spirit of that person—he has, in fact, what is, for him, unquestionable proof of immortality. The Bantus believe that the spirits of the dead manifest themselves and communicate in dreams ; and the same definite belief is found in the case of many primitive races : as, for example, among the Andaman Islanders, the Veddas of Ceylon, the Dieri and Buandik of South-East Australia (all of them people very low in the scale of humanity), and the Marshall Islanders. Roscoe tells us that among one of the Uganda tribes (the Basabei) " Dreams were regarded as conversations with the ghosts, who took this means of warning and advising their living relatives." And it should be remembered that, in nearly all primitive societies, the ghost is expected, and most dreaded, at night—the time when people sleep and dream. It is in the dark that ghostly activities are most pronounced, and in the dark that apparitions of the dead are most frequently seen or imagined. It is possible, too, that the contemplation of sleep or trance or any form of unconsciousness, and of the return to the fully awakened state, may have contributed towards the belief.

In Scotch superstition, to dream of the dead was a sign that they were not at rest : the dream was an actual visitation. The records of psychic research contain innumerable cases of the appearance of the dead or dying in dreams, and not infrequently such visions are alleged to foretell the death of the dreamer, or of some person known to him. It is also very widely believed, that the soul of a living person may leave the body during sleep, and that it may then encounter, and hold converse with, the souls either of the living or the departed. A dream in which the wraith of a dead person is apparently met by the dreamer has a peculiar vividness and significance, and even if dreams of this type do not entirely account for the original belief in ghosts, they do at any rate offer an explanation which has certain advantages. The most wretchedly primitive folk have an unquestioning faith in the survival of the human spirit : whatever may be the sources of that faith it is clear that they will be found in the common observation and experience of the primitive mind, and it is here that dreams may be assumed to play a very important part.

Having formed a belief in human immortality as a result of some common and repeated experience which, at a low level of primitive culture, might easily form the basis of such a belief, it is not to be wondered at that primitive man should evolve certain ideas concerning the nature of the soul, and its fate in the after-life. Those ideas, on account of their strangeness and diversity, are of great interest.

THE NATURE OF THE SOUL, ACCORDING TO PRIMITIVE MAN

The natives of Australia, a people so low in the scale of mental development that they had not even approached the god-making stage, believed, generally, that the soul left the body at death, and, after a sojourn in the land of spirits, was reborn in a human being. But one tribe, the Gnanji, believed that the soul which occupied the body of a woman perished when the woman died. It would appear that the size of the soul awaiting reincarnation was exceedingly small ; it was described as no larger than a grain of sand when, at the conclusion of the lengthy and extraordinary funeral rites of the Warramunga tribe, it set out for the spirit-home. The Pennefather natives thought that there was a second soul called the *ngai*, which resided in the heart, and at death passed immediately into the children of the deceased. The Buandik believed that each man possessed two indwelling spirits : at death one went down into the sea, to return again as a white man, and the other ascended to the clouds. The Bigambul, convinced that the soul could freely leave the body during life, thought of death as a state which forbade the return of the soul, thus identifying it with the vital principle. In the case of the Ngarigo we have a curious instance of a belief in ghostly disability which is very widely distributed, and still exists in Europe ; for the Ngarigo funeral party, after the burial, were careful to cross a river, in order that the ghost might be unable to follow them.

The Tami of New Guinea are of opinion that man possesses two souls ; a short one and a long one. The long soul is identified with the shadow, and apparently takes part in the experience of dreams ; the short soul does not leave the body until death, when, after hovering for a while near the corpse, it proceeds to Lamboam, the realm of spirits. Another New Guinea tribe, the Wind-essi, also believe in two souls : when a woman dies, both her spirits go down to the nether world, but one of the two souls of a man may pass into another man, who thus acquires unusual and mysterious gifts. Among the Solomon Islanders a firm distinction is made between powerful ghosts (those of strong or important men) and feeble ghosts (those of the puny or insignificant), and a similar distinction occurs frequently. The Tongans, for example, were persuaded that the spirits of their nobles were promoted, after death, to something like divine rank ; the spirits of less important folk also went to the abode of the blessed, but did not cut much of a figure there ; while commoners had no souls at all, or souls made of such poor and attenuated stuff that they perished with the body. According to Dr. C. E. Fox, the people of San Cristoval, in the Solomon Islands, believed that a man had two souls : the one called *adaro*, the shadow-soul, was malevolent ; the other, *aunga*, likened to a reflection in water, was kindly and quiet. The head was apparently regarded as the seat of the vital principle, and the *adaro* might enter the skull after death. But the *aunga*, though dwelling specially in the head, permeated the whole body, and even extended to a person's clothes, food, and intimate property. The *aunga* generally left the body, and it might do so during life, through the top of the head, but sometimes by the mouth, nose, ears, or navel. After a man's death, it was his *adaro* or malicious soul which was feared and placated by the survivors. Among the Samoans there were some who could see the soul at the moment of death : it was of the same shape as the body, and its appearance was greatly dreaded. The Society Islanders held that the spirits of the dead had knowledge of future events, and that they would obligingly convey that knowledge to the living : they thought that the spirit of a man resided in his bowels. The Hawaiians believed that the soul was located in the eye-sockets " and above all in the lachrymal gland " (Frazer), and they also believed in a dual soul, rather similar to that of the New Guinea Tami.

A very singular instance of the dual soul is to be found in the case of the Bagobo of the Philippines. These people consider that there is a soul on each side of the body ; the left soul is a vagrant, good-for-nothing creature, wandering from the body during sleep, and after death becoming an evil spirit, bringing sickness and misfortunes on men ; but the right soul is well-disposed, gentle, and virtuous, sticks to the body and takes care of it, and at death joins the great company of ancestors in the underworld.

In Dutch Borneo, the apparition of an *antu* or spirit may be of gigantic size. The soul, however, does not live eternally : it dies and revives three or even seven times, and at last, thin and vapourish, disperses foggily in the atmosphere and comes to an end.

According to W. J. Perry, the Toradja of Celebes conceive of the soul as a little replica of its owner, or as a shadow. It can leave the body by the top of the head or by the mouth, nose, ears, or joints. It can assume various shapes after leaving the body; in proof of which we are told how, when two Toradja men were sleeping in a hut, one of them saw a mouse run out of the other's nose—he killed it, and then perceived that his companion was dead. In some of its animal forms the soul can devour other souls. But here again we seem to have a case of duality, for we are told that there is a distinction between soul and ghost, and that the former does not pass to the land of the dead. The soul or "soul-stuff" is apparently connected with the breath.

From the former, if not the present, practice of the Gilbert Islanders we see that these people did not consider that a child was born with a soul. For some days after the birth of a child, the near relatives danced assiduously round a bonfire; presumably in order to attract the attention of some wandering soul and to show it the whereabouts of a new lodging. These Islanders identified the soul with the shadow, and thought that after death it hovered near the body for three days, and then ascended into the air, where it was blown about by the breezes; finally it passed to a typical Island paradise. The Marshall Islanders appear to have thought of the spirit of man as something quick-moving, transparent, and fluid.

In Africa, where the cult of the dead is often so grimly associated with dark and bloody ritual, we find the most amazing diversity of views—from a seemingly absolute denial of immortality to the most complex and detailed accounts of the spiritual elements and of the life after death. The Bari are supposed to deny the survival of the spirit; and Schweinfurth said that "The Bongo have not the remotest conception of immortality," though he wrote later, with strange inconsistency, "Quite amazing is the fear which exists among the Bongo about ghosts, whose abode is said to be in the shadowy

darkness of the woods." The Masai and Bahima regard
immortality as a kingly or aristocratic privilege, withheld from common people. Belief in duality, or even
plurality of souls is essentially a characteristic of many
African religions. In West Africa there is a widespread
belief in the soul of the body and the soul of the spirit.
The Tshi-speaking people have a curious notion about a
spirit called the *kra*, which enters the body at birth and
leaves it at death, and is not in any way connected with
the personal soul. Another group maintains that each
body is tenanted by a male soul which is bad and violent,
and by a female soul which is gentle and good. Among
the Yoruba it is thought that a man has three indwelling
spirits ; one in his head, one in his stomach, and one in
his big toe. The Hausa of Nigeria and the Bavili of the
Northern Congo both affirm the existence of a quadruple
spiritual nature : soul, shadow, life, and double. The
peculiar part of the Hausa conception consists in the
supposed nature of the " double," which looks exactly
like the person to whom it belongs but is always outside
him. Beliefs in two, three, or four spiritual elements
are found among other African peoples, and the Bambula
allege that there is a fifth element, only to be found in
very bad people, and incorrigibly wicked, even after
death.

The Ibo, a Nigerian tribe, considered that the spirit
of a man could enter inanimate things, but that the
spirit of an animal could not. This belief in the souls of
animals (for which there was a special Elysium) was not
shared by the Bantus, who stated definitely that cattle
had no *ngoma* or soul, though they might be possessed
temporarily by a human *ngoma*. The human spirit was
identified with the breath, and its character when disembodied was exactly similar to that of the living man.
Among the Banyankole, it was considered that the
ghosts of women might be of special danger to the women
and children of their own tribe. But the ghosts of women,

in primitive African thought, receive, as a rule, very
little attention ; and this is the case elsewhere.

In Dahomey, the ghost of a king was able, in some
mysterious way, to occupy more than one place at the
same time : thus, at the So-sin Custom held in honour
of Gézu by his son and successor, Gézu was in his taber-
nacle, on his war-stool, and in his ghost-mother at one
and the same moment—and he might also have been
reincarnate in some member of the royal family. In
parts of Central Africa, the kingly ghost may enter a lion,
or some other formidable beast. The people of Ashanti
said that the soul was like the wind ; and it was thought
that the disembodied ghost could injure folk by touching
them. (The association of the spirits of the dead with
the wind is frequent in Africa. In Irish folklore, the
presence of the spirits of the dead or of ghostly agencies
may be indicated by a blast of wind. An Aran woman
told Lady Gregory : "Sometimes they travel like a
cloud or like a storm." The same conception appears in
Greek thought, where the winds are associated with
underworld gods and with the dead.)

Although the Eskimo have not produced a religious
system they seem to have very definite ideas about the
soul. According to Rasmussen, they believe that the
individual consists of a body, a soul, and a name-soul.
The soul proper, like the " double " of the Nigerian
Hausa, is outside the body, and moves about with it like
a shadow ; it is the exact counterpart of the person
to whom it belongs, but is smaller. The soul is visible
to magicians ; it may, indeed, be stolen by some
malicious wizard and buried in a hole in the snow : a
person whose soul is thus stolen will die quickly unless
it can be found (also by a wizard) and restored to its
owner. "Originally," we are told, " the Eskimo
regarded the name as a kind of soul, with which was
associated a certain amount of vitality and dexterity."
A man named after the deceased inherited his qualities,

and the dead man was not at rest until his name had been handed on. After death, the name-soul entered a pregnant woman and was born with her child, but it could only be identified by a magician.

North American Indian beliefs appear to have been rather similar to those of the Eskimo. The Chippewa called the soul O'chechag, and said that it quitted the body during trance or unconsciousness. Animals, and even inanimate things, had souls.

But the teaching of animism, which looks on the human soul as only one among innumerable other kinds of soul, reached one of its fullest developments in primitive China. The primitive Chinese had a most exciting, a most exuberant faith in the ghostly. To their thinking, the soul of man was composed of the *yang* and the *yin*; the light and good, and the dark and bad elements of the universe. After death, immense numbers of souls banded together, and by their wicked activities utterly maddened and demoralised whole provinces. Objects had souls : coffin-lids flew through the air, frightening people and knocking them down ; pots and pans chattered in the dark ; rotten wood and old brooms were incendiary spectres ; the phantasms of flying objects emitted a smell of decay, and if touched were found to be soft and slippery. In short, the Chinaman lived in the midst of a fast and furious world of energetic and mischievous ghosts ; and as though ghosts of his own kind were not bad enough, he was liable to be beset and bedevilled by the phantoms of animals, bricks, kettles, and broomsticks.

In this necessarily curtailed survey of primitive ideas concerning the nature and composition of the soul I have only been able to select such instances as might serve to prepare the reader for the diversity of opinions of which we shall find evidence again and again in the course of our study, and such as might lead him to anticipate and understand the many strange views on the subject of immortality which we are about to consider. The next step in our enquiry is to examine primitive teaching and belief in regard to the destiny of the soul after its final departure from the body.

ESCHATOLOGY: THE FATE OF THE SOUL

" Many have taken voluminous pains to determine the state of the soul upon disunion," wrote Sir Thomas Browne. Many indeed have been the essays of faith and speculation upon this momentous theme, and too many, alas! have been the frauds and cruelties, the pitiable tricks and vulgar impostures, which have centred upon it in modern times. But it must be remembered, that although the subject of the after-life is one on which the majority of civilised mankind have few clear and settled opinions, it is a subject that presents no great difficulties to the primitive thinker. Primitive man, on his mystic side, is usually amazingly definite. With him, believing is knowing. Let us therefore refrain from despising the poor heathen : perhaps he possesses something that we do not possess ; and knows something that we do not know—or have forgotten.

Primitive eschatology assumes that one or the other of the following destinies awaits the soul of a person who has died in ordinary circumstances : (a) it proceeds, generally with an escort, to a judgment-hall, and is thenceforth doomed to an eternity of pains or pleasures, or consigned to utter destruction ; (b) it sets out by itself for the land of spirits, and often has to escape ambushes and dodge demons before it can get there ; its good or evil conduct while on earth may, but probably does not, influence its fate on this journey ; (c) it moves to an island, a cavern, or a wood, not far from its earthly home, where it lives with other ghosts and pays occasional

visits to its relations ; (d) it hangs about in the neighbourhood of its tomb or house, and is always in close
touch with the people of the tribe or village ; if it can
outlive the normal period of memory it is in a fair way
to attaining divine honours ; (e) it remains in attendance
on the body, or on parts of the body, during the funeral
rites and the mourning (perhaps for as long as two years),
and is then forcibly expelled to the land of the dead,
whence it never returns ; (f) it is reborn, or enters the
body of another person, immediately or soon after death.
Exceptions are often made in the cases of murdered men,
suicides, people killed by animals, people whose bodies
are not properly buried, women who die in childbirth,
and very young children. It is hardly ever believed that
the behaviour of a person on earth has anything whatever to do with the conditions of his life in the hereafter.
On the contrary, no matter how detestable he may have
been, his ghost is at liberty to scare the survivors out
of their senses, or even to kill them, if they do not
mourn for him and bury him in the approved fashion.
That the soul continues to live indefinitely, or in one
state, is not by any means the general opinion.

We shall now pass in review a number of typical
examples of primitive teaching.

On the high country in the south of India there lives
an exceedingly primitive people called the Todas. The
book which has been written about these folk by
W. H. R. Rivers is a pattern of anthropological thorough-
ness, and from that book I take the following account
of the Toda eschatology :—Amnòdr, the other world,
lies to the west, and is lighted by the sun after it has
set on the Nilgiri Hills. But although lighted by the
sun, it is below the level of the earth ; and that is why
the Toda dead were formerly buried face downward.
Amnòdr is ruled by the god On. The spirits of the dead
spend their time there very much as they did while
among the living, and are kept busy with their buffaloes

and dairies. But they suffer from a strange inconveni-
ence. Continual walking about wears away their legs,
and at last they have nothing to serve them but a pair
of miserable stumps. At this stage, On sends them back
to this world as new and properly constructed people.
The dead travel to Amnòdr by definite routes : there is
a stone called hot-knock-stone on which the ghosts
bump themselves, and so lose all hankering after the
earthly life ; and another stone called Panipikârs,
against which they also bump, and become sound and
vigorous. Then they go through a wood, and each
ghost makes a cut on a tree with the knife which was
burnt with his body. After that, they come to a river
spanned by a bridge of thread, and there those who have
led bad lives fall into the water and are bitten by
leeches ; but they scramble out, it appears, and join
the rest.

In this case, the punishment for earthly misdeeds is a
mere pretence—no worse than might befall one on an
afternoon's walk in the country. As a rule, however,
earthly misdeeds are not taken into account at all. The
Gilbert Islanders provide a notable exception, for they
believe that the punishment for sin is everlasting
torment : a conception which almost places these people
on a level with civilised man.

The Australian natives have paid their invaders the
compliment of assuming that the best white men are
probably the souls of black-fellows, returned in a new
and improved form ; but some believe that the soul
ascends to the sky, whence it may occasionally descend
to visit old comrades, sometimes to tease and at others
to help. The Wotjo maintain that the ghost stays near
the grave for a considerable time, and the Wiradjuri
say that it haunts the place where it has lived in the
body, and takes up its abode in a large tree. The Bigambul think that the shades of the dead go about much
as they did when in the flesh. Belief in the Alcheringa,

the great realm of spirit-land where the souls wait until their time for reincarnation, is general among the northern tribes.

In Maori belief, the soul lingered near the body for three days after death. Some Maoris were of opinion that the spirit remained always near the place where the body was buried or where its relics were preserved; others maintained that the ghost ascended or descended to the world of shades; while yet others believed that the souls of common folk went down to the deepest and darkest of regions, wriggling back to the surface of the earth in the form of worms and perishing, while the souls of important men rose to the skies.

The Koita of British New Guinea believe that the spirit after death goes to a mountain called Idu, but that it only lives for a certain time. The Mafalu also believe that the spirit ascends to the mountains, where it takes the form either of a soft light or of a big fungus. The Monumbo hold that the spirits of the dead grow old and die, and are then changed to animals or plants. New Caledonians, good and bad alike, pass after death to the fairest imaginable land at the bottom of the sea, north-east of the island of Pott: here they spend their nights of sleepless joy, and by day they resort to the cemeteries. The Melanesian ghost, generally speaking, makes his way to the islands of the dead, but he returns at times to the neighbourhood of his grave, and makes himself both seen and heard.

The Fijians had no liking for the bachelor. Not only was the poor man despised and slighted during his life-time, but his miserable ghost, feebly yet hopefully wandering towards the land of the blessed, was seized and devoured by a hobgoblin. But no one had an easy journey to paradise: trials and monsters awaited the travelling soul, and only the hardiest reached the happy land where, it seems, the successful murderer was the most richly rewarded of all. The Society Islanders held various beliefs : the soul after death entered a wooden image ; or it went to a gloomy region where the gods lived ; or it was " converted into a piece of furniture resembling an English hatstand" (Frazer). The Hawaiians, also, were not of one mind : in general, they believed that the souls of the illustrious rose to the heavens above, while the souls of ordinary folk descended below the earth to a humble place where they regaled themselves on lizards and butterflies.

In the opinion of the natives of Dutch Borneo, the spirit of a deceased person may build itself a ghostly invisible nest in a swaying tree-top—a shadowy rock-a-bye baby—or it may wander on the hills. After leaving the body at death, souls have to cross, or get round, a hill of fire ; the good ones are cunning, and find out how to escape the flames, but the bad ones go lumbering over the hill and are horribly burnt—however, they are only hurt for a time, not destroyed. Again, the un-civilised notion of limited punishment.

The Dyaks share with the Dutch Borneo people the belief that the ghost, in time, grows thin and filmy, and is finally drawn into the upper air and dissolved in dews and fogs. The Ballaus think that the spirit-world is beneath the earth, and is divided into a happy place, where living people and ghosts hob-nob together, and a gloomy region, inhabited only by the sulky shades of the dead ; while the Sibuyows believe that man has seven lives, of which the earthly life is the first, and the seventh is in heaven—a well-planned town, full of con-veniences and amusements (Ling Roth). The Dusuns held that the souls of the dead went up Mount Kinabalu ; and any mortals who climbed the mountain thought it polite and proper to warn the ghosts of their coming by means of gunfire.

That the spirits ascended to the mountains was a com-mon belief in other parts of Indonesia. In Watubela, the ghosts went to live on a mountain in east Seran ;

and in Seran, commoners, after death, took up their abode in the high hills. In Minabassa (Celebes) ghosts of notables go up to the sky, and those of the lower orders wander in the forest (W. J. Perry).

The body of a dead person in the Marshall Islands was sewn up in a mat and buried in the earth, and for six days after the burial the spirit remained in the grave with this melancholy package ; then it flitted to the isle of Narikrik, where it had to avoid a demon, and so passed to Eorerok, the island of Shades. It approached Eorerok in the form either of a big or of a little canoe, according to its merit or importance ; and there were those on the shore who awaited its coming, and gave judgment. The soul of the departed Mortlock Islander (Carolines) took the form of a sea-bird, and if it was a good soul it was led to heaven under divine guidance. But the bad soul was cast into a welter of abominations, destined to utter destruction at the last judgment : a teaching which could scarcely be improved on by the white missionary.

Sir J. G. Frazer tells us that the Yap Islanders have two theories about the life of the invisible personality after death : either it becomes idiotic, or it remains in full possession of its wits and intelligence. The soul lingers near the body until the latter has decayed (a most frequent belief in all parts of the world, and apparently one of extreme antiquity), and then goes to live in a sort of ghostly lodging-house called Falraman. From this place it is free to revisit its old home, and, if it finds them slack in the performance of the mourning rites, to bring sickness and disaster on its living relatives. It is not surprising, therefore, to find that the relations of the recently departed take good care to worship and propitiate the ghost in the house which it has occupied during its earthly life. The ghost appears to the living as a glimmering cockchafer.

It is very widely believed that the soul remains in

close attendance on the body for some time after death. The Cheyenne Indians buried the bodies of their dead as speedily as possible, in order that the ghost might be soon removed from the neighbourhood of the living. The ghost of the Huron Indian walked with the funeral party to the burial place, and remained in the cemetery until the great feast of the dead, when the bones or bodies of the deceased were reverently disinterred and placed in a common grave : then, if the ghost was a sturdy one, it set out on its long journey towards the setting sun. During its residence in the cemetery it would sometimes visit the wigwams, take part in social events, and eat what was left in the food-kettles. According to the Iroquois, the journey of the soul from earth to heaven lasted a whole year ; and they believed that the soul hovered near the body until it was ready to take its departure. A fire was often lighted on the grave, so that the spirit might be able to cook its meals. The Chippewa believed that animals and things had souls, and that men who had injured them would be plagued by their phantasms in the after-life. But the good and gentle Chippewa people would spend their eternity in dancing, singing, and eating mushrooms. In Eskimo belief, the soul either ascended to heaven or went down into the sea, but it was equally pleasant in both places. The Maya Indians of Yucatan held, in common with many other peoples, that the air was full of *pishan* or souls of the dead.

This conviction, that the ghosts of the dead throng about the habitations of the living, that they are with us at all times, though chiefly at night, and in some way dependent on our care and hospitality, is strongly held by the peasants of Brittany. Indeed, this belief is so well exhibited in Breton superstition, it is so essentially a primitive form of belief, comparatively free from any infusion or tincture of modern religious thought, that we shall not do wrong in classifying the Breton, and some of his neighbours, among those primitive folk whose opinions we are describing.

The Keltic teaching is, fundamentally, that the next life, in all its circumstances, is an exact repetition of the present one ; the same joys, the same cares and needs await the ghost ; and he moves over the same ground, in the same houses, and among the same people with whom he was familiar in the flesh. Le Braz, speaking of the dead Breton, says : " *Sa maison, il la hante presque autant que par le passé. It revient s'asseoir dans l'âtre, chauffer ses pieds à la braise.*" In Brittany, the dead are usually invisible by day, but they are not absent ; at night they are everywhere, passing silently along the highways or across the fields, and entering the houses. So, in order that they may be assured of a welcome and provided with food and warmth, the house-holder is careful to leave his door unbolted when he retires to bed, careful to leave his fire glowing, and victuals on the table ; neither is the good wife allowed to ply her broom too busily in the evening, for she might sweep away some poor ghostly guest who has crept in for a little comfort. And lying upstairs a-bed, both man and wife may hear the stirring and shuffling of the ghosts in the kitchen below them.

As a concession—and practically the only concession —to Catholic dogma, the soul is dispatched to the heavenly tribunal immediately after death, to receive its particular judgment ; but this is no sooner given than it comes posting back to the body. At this stage (and we have seen the same idea elsewhere) the soul is thought of as some minute and fragile thing : it may tumble into a jug of milk and get drowned, or it may be dusted away. Sometimes it is seen in the form of a fly or a mouse. But it is clear that, after the burial, the ghost takes on its recognisable human form, and it may even become solid and corporeal—working in the fields, riding horses, knocking people down, playing skittles, and so on. There is, indeed, an amazing story of a *revenant* actually begetting a child. Those who die a premature or violent death remain in some kind of intermediate state until a space of time equal to that of the completed normal life has passed. Those who are drowned at sea and whose bodies are not recovered wander for ever along the coast, crying dismally : Iou ! Iou ! Children who die before baptism wander in the air as birds : other souls expiate their sins in the likeness of a cow or bull, according to the sex of the sinner. Great landowners haunt their ruined châteaux in the form of hares ; and it is said that a woman who died after killing her seven bastards became a sow with a litter of seven little pigs.

There are three great festivals of the dead in Brittany, at all of which the cold and hungry ghosts take part in the ceremonial and share in the feast : Christmas Eve, St. John's Eve, and All Saint's Eve. On Christmas Eve, religious processions are formed, led by an old, emaciated priest and a little choir-boy ; and while these processions move along the roads and the village streets, great companies of drowned men move on the surface of the sea—ghostly companies, in procession also, keeping pace, all grey and silent, with those on land. St. John's Eve is a festival of bonfires, and at these fires the clustering ghosts warm themselves, for they are always chilly. At the festival of All Saint's Eve, the people visit the charnel houses after vespers and sing a peculiar chant known as the *gwerz*. After this they go home, prepare the tables, whereon they set food and drink of the best, and make up great roaring fires on the hearths, so that the dead may have good cheer and comfort. Soon after nine in the evening the death-singers go on their rounds, chanting the mournful complaint of the ghosts, and it is then that the folk who have gone early to bed hear strange sounds, and know that their guests have arrived. At dawn, the dead and the living make their way together to the parish church, and listen to a requiem.

The cult of the dead is not strongly developed among the Welsh people, and they have no distinctive views on eschatology. It was believed, in some parts of Wales, that a spirit named Margan conducted the soul to the other world, and that the dead reappeared invariably on the ninth day after death.

In Ireland, the living are in close, if not continual, relations with the dead. The fairies of Connemara and the spirits of the departed keep company together. I think it is very probable that the fairies themselves, together with the Sidhe and the Tuatha de Danaan (associated as they are with dolmens and burial mounds, with chapels and churchyards) are ghosts of more ancient date. Like the Bretons, the Irish believe in the ghostly population of the seas : Lady Gregory tells of an old man who was submerged in his boat by the power of invisible hands, and who declared that " he had never seen so many people as he did in that minute under the water." And like many other primitive dreamers they maintain that it is possible for the soul, and for body and soul together, to visit the realms of the dead and to return again to the living. In this case, it seems evident that the regions of the Sidhe and of departed spirits are confounded ; for it is occasionally said of one who has fallen sick and died that he was taken " by *them* "—i.e., the Sidhe. There are stories of dead wives returning to their husbands, and being prevented from leaving the house by force ; such home-comings may occur as late as seven years after the death. It is commonly alleged that the dead are seen " walking " soon after their burial. That they reappear always in human form is uncertain, for the flight of a company of ghosts has been likened to a flight of birds. The cordial welcome accorded to the Breton ghost has no parallel in Ireland, though it was formerly the custom to place some griddle cakes or potatoes outside the house for a few nights after a death had taken place : a slightly better provision than that made by the Scotch, who considered that a drink of water was as much as the poor ghost had any right to expect.

We have already cited the Andaman Islanders as an exceedingly primitive people, and their views on the after-life are therefore of much interest. But those views, according to A. R. Brown, whose excellent book on the Islanders is the accepted source of information, are not consistent, and are marked by a certain vagueness. Their very inconsistency, however, is interesting, for it shows us a number of ideas which are characteristic of primitive thought. The Aka-Kede believe that when a man dies he becomes a spirit and goes to the spirit-world under the earth, where he is ceremoniously initiated and introduced by those who have arrived there already. That is a clear belief, but such clarity is rare, and Mr. Brown tells us : " Whenever I asked the natives whence came the spirits of the jungle and the sea I received the answer that they are the spirits of dead men and women. On the other hand, when I put in another form what might seem to be the same question, and asked what became of a man's spirit after his death, I received many different and inconsistent answers." The northern tribes think that when a man has died his spirit goes wandering in the jungle, at first keeping near the grave, and eventually joining up with the other spirits. The ghost, however, stays in his own country —a parochial restriction which is very commonly observed by ghosts in all parts of the world. Another account has it that the spirit at death, or soon after, goes to Maramika, the lower world, which is exactly like the upper world ; and yet another account maintains that the spirits go up to an abode in the sky. It is believed here, and it is, as I have said, an idea that occurs again and again in primitive thought, that the ghost is

not able to take its final flight until the flesh of the body
has entirely rotted away from the bones. A member
of one of the southern tribes told A. R. Brown that the
spirit goes over the edge of the world to a place called
Spirit's House, where it leads the same kind of life that
it has led already in the flesh ; and according to another
informant the journeying soul was subject both to
devious wanderings and to severe trials before Spirit's
House was reached. The southern tribes also believe
that souls ascend to the realm of Tomo, a being sometimes regarded as the first ancestor : here they have as
much pork and turtle as they can possibly desire, and
spend their time very pleasantly. The ghosts of medicinemen are distinguished from those of ordinary persons,
with whom they have nothing in common ; they take
an active part in human affairs, controlling the weather
and causing or curing sickness.

An even more primitive folk, the Veddas of Ceylon,
while vague as to the particulars of the next life, believe
that the soul does not acquire its full privileges until
a few days after death.

Modern African beliefs vary, but do not differ greatly
from those of other uncivilised peoples. Royal souls
are well received in Deadland, and are kept in touch
with all that is going on in their earthly kingdoms by
means of messengers—slaves who are ceremonially
decapitated, or otherwise killed, and thus dispatched
with news to the underworld. Here, again, the shades
of the dead return to move among the living ; but they
are regarded, for the most part, with terror, and no one
is anxious to meet or entertain them. Immortality is
frequently conditioned by rank or power, and many
African souls do not survive the death of the body. In
Central Africa, ghosts are often regarded as friendly or
malevolent in accordance with their treatment by the
living: if well treated they are kind and helpful, but if neglected they become a source of danger. The Banyankole

of all classes had shrines for the family ghosts, where milk was offered daily—not ordinary milk, but the milk of cows dedicated specially to this holy service. It is a fairly general belief in the Uganda Protectorate that, although ghosts have a localised residence, they spend most of their time among the living; haunting, or even taking up a prolonged abode in, the places which were dear to them during their life on earth.

Such are a few of the more typical primitive doctrines concerning the fate of the soul. It will be noted that the idea of retributive justice is generally absent; that a person's lot in the hereafter is often assumed to be conditioned by his rank and influence on earth; that the ghost is commonly thought of as in close attendance on the body for some time after death, and that its movements after death may be confined to a given locality; but most important of all, that death, instead of cancelling all relations between the living and the departed, merely places those relations under another aspect. The question of intercourse between this world and the next is so intimately connected with the question of the fate of the soul, that it seems necessary, at this stage, to examine the general form of the answers to that question which have been advanced by early or primitive thought.

RELATION BETWEEN THE DEAD AND THE LIVING

The belief in immortality has not proved an unmixed blessing to mankind. Many of its results have been truly deplorable. It has given rise to religious exercises so fanatical and bloody, to a despotism of the dead so terrible in action, that life, in parts of the primitive world, has been made almost unendurable for the living. Indeed, the ghastly exactions of cult or the mere dread of the vengeance of the ghost have seriously restricted the numbers of the living in certain districts, and have

sometimes threatened the complete extinction of a race.
Even where matters were not carried to these horrible
extremes, the assumed posthumous existence of the
dead was more often a scourge than a consolation to the
survivors ; and the least offensive habit of the deceased
was to maintain an exact and relentless system of espionage. This espionage enabled the ghost to inflict condign
punishment for any transgressions against the tribal
codes and particularly for any failure to observe the
dues of the dead. Not only the great communal disasters,
but all the ordinary mishaps of life were caused by the
mischievous interference, the jealousy, or the revenge
of the deceased.

The primitive conception of ghosts would appear to
start off with the idea that they are more or less
malevolent in their relations with the living ; freakish
and spiteful, if not downright deadly. Once a man had
passed from the earthly life he had unlimited oppor-
tunities for wiping off old scores, and for plaguing his
former companions for the mere fun of the thing. He
was not above the most childish practical jokes : pop-
ping up in unexpected places, whistling, squeaking,
and taking delight in all sorts of silly but exasperating
tricks. In fact, the human ghost was usually regarded
as a being whose chief concern was to be troublesome,
to frighten people and to do them harm.

And yet, it is not easy to say, at first glance, whether
the general attitude of primitive men towards their
dead is compounded entirely of fear, with no trace of
affection. Fear and affection may represent co-existent
aspects of a strongly realised personal relationship ; it
might perhaps be said that they represent two elements
which are invariably present in every human relationship. So it is not surprising to find that a most tender
regard for the welfare of the dead may be coupled with
an abject terror of the ghost, and with a desire to prevent
its appearance or to scare it away if it does appear. That,

indeed, is the attitude of many civilised men. And it is certain, that although the element of affection is not always discernible in the primitive attitude towards the dead, the element of fear is always discernible, in greater or lesser intensity. A powerful or wicked person is especially dreaded after his death, but a mild and peaceful person is dreaded also : hence, it is something in the actual state of ghostliness which inspires fear. There is no difficulty in finding an explanation. The ghost, since he is able to move and to strike in secrecy and in silence, since he may gain admission to your house whenever and however he pleases, is not to be trusted. The kindest of ghosts cannot resist the temptation to disconcert you and to make your flesh creep. You can tell where you are, more or less, with a living man, and if he is too troublesome you can imprison him ; but you cannot reckon with a ghost, you cannot impound it.

Professor Petrie has argued that the predynastic Egyptians must have regarded their dead with affection, not with fear ; because they provided them with valuable things and with weapons. That does not follow. Armed with all the resources of ghostly power, able to make himself known and felt both in the world of dreams and in the world of reality, the dead man had little need of material weapons. Moreover, holding back the cherished property of the deceased is asking for the worst kind of trouble. We find deposits of weapons or the provision of an armed escort among races whose feelings towards the dead are those of unmitigated fear and continual apprehension.

That the dead exercise an unceasing influence, baleful or benevolent as the case may be, on the affairs of the living, is an absolute conviction with the great majority of the primitive races of to-day. On this subject they have no doubt whatsoever. It is a thing as evident to their senses as the brightness of the sun or the power of the wind or the cycle of growth and decay. The only difference—and it is a terrifying difference—between the action of a living person and the action of a spirit is, that the spirit has immeasurably greater powers for good or for evil. And since the spirit retains his human attributes, he generally finds it more amusing to use his powers for evil. The general tendency, beyond doubt, is to believe that the disembodied spirit regards the living with malice, with an exultant sense of superiority, but yet with bitterness, and with a jealous insistence on its own prerogatives. Speaking of the Central Melanesians, Sir J. G. Frazer has observed : " To him the belief [in immortality] is no mere abstract theological dogma or speculative tenet . . . it is an inbred, unquestioning, omnipresent conviction which affects his thoughts and actions daily and at every turn ; it guides his fortunes as an individual and controls his behaviour as a member of a community." Such " omnipresent conviction," with its natural effects on individual conduct, distinguishes all the primitive forms of faith.

Since he is continually spied upon by powerful beings who are generally hostile, or at least mischievous, visible or invisible at will, and able to move in defiance of all those laws by which corporate man is himself restrained, the " savage " is careful to keep on the right side of his departed neighbours. It may be that his own family ghosts are less dangerous to him than those of strangers ; but he dreads them all. When his relatives die, he often inflicts the most dolorous injuries on himself, in order that the ghost may not be able to reproach him with indifference. Nor is this all, for he may severely belabour, or even kill, any of his kin who are backward in this respect ; since it is well known that the slighted ghost does not trouble to make distinctions, but falls foul of every one within his reach.

Leaving the religions of civilised peoples out of account (though I doubt whether they should really be excepted), it is but rarely that the ghost of a dead person is regarded as a trustworthy friend. I know that the pious Greek, opening the wine jars on the first day of the Dionysian feast of souls, the Anthesteria, made a pretence of extending a welcome to the family shades ; but he did this only because he was anxious to keep them well disposed, or quiet, and he was not slow in showing them the door. I know that the dead are sometimes buried close to the house or the hearth, or even beneath the floor on which the family lives ; but that is done because the ghost, not wandering far from its former dwelling, may be the more easily controlled or propitiated. The primeval attitude of fear may occasionally, perhaps through sheer exasperation, be exchanged for one of defiance. Instead of grovelling, the afflicted survivors may speak to the ghost with firm or even threatening accents : " Come, you are dead now. Be at peace. Anyhow, let us see no more of you : leave us alone, and do not come back to injure us or our children. We have done all that is proper for your welfare, and you have no further claim on us." But there is hardly a single instance in which primitive man looks on his dead as necessarily well disposed and affectionate. Indeed, it is probable that a close examination of the facts may lead us to the conclusion that such an instance does not exist. The desire to enter into friendly relations with the dead does not imply the belief that the dead themselves are moved by a corresponding impulse, any more than the worship of a god implies a belief in his essential amiability. The friendship of the dead may be gained : it is rarely, if ever, taken for granted.

We are told that, when a king of Benin died, his favourites and retainers vied with each other for the privilege of being buried alive with the body. We are assured that in other parts of Africa, and elsewhere, voluntary immolation, on such occasions, was frequent. At first glance, we might suspect an extraordinary degree of affection for the deceased. But on looking into the matter, we find, first, that public opinion was a potent factor in such cases, and that the lives of the surviving associates of a king were made wellnigh intolerable by the succeeding courtiers ; and second, that the dead ruler himself was a menace to all concerned if he was not duly accompanied by his willing wives and by servants who were acquainted with his ways and requirements. There are actually cases in which the good will of important folk has been solicited before their death ; as in ancient China, where the spiritual part of a great man was assumed to reside, during his lifetime, in various portrait-images, which received offerings and reverence and were entertained by puppet shows. Among many races whose simple faith is yet unassailed, people try to get on the right side of the ghost before it leaves the body, and they do so by bringing presents to the dying man. But this is where a knowledge of the ghostly comes in, for it is understood that the departed spirit cannot make use of the substance of the gifts : the offerings are purely symbolic, and, after death has occurred, all the things are taken away by the donors.

All this points to the fact that immortality is often regarded by unsophisticated people as a prolongation of the earthly life ; and moreover, a prolongation on the earth itself, and in touch with living men. The haunting or visiting ghost, though he may have his own quarters in some distant spirit-land, spends a great deal if not most of his time among his old associates.

These ghostly visitations are seldom appreciated by the living, and in the case of civilised communities, religion and scepticism between them have made things extremely difficult for the spectre ; for the one teaches his safe relegation to a region from whence return is not permitted, and the other questions his very existence —so that any poor ghost who ventures to come back finds that it is no easy matter to get a hearing. One of the most awful curses of ghostliness in a civilised

country must be to find yourself regarded as a hallucination—gently explained away by some obstinate scientist.
But the primitive man has no scientist to explain away,
no church to exorcise ; he has to put up with the ghost
and to make the best of him.

DEATH-DEALERS

Although death leads to and reveals the splendours,
the powers and the advantages of immortality, death is
but seldom looked on as desirable, as a thing to be loved
or courted. On the contrary, it is a very widespread
belief among the uncivilised that people would not die
at all if they were not destroyed by the evil spells of their
enemies. The death from sickness of a man in the prime
of life is often bloodily avenged on the members of the
clan or village who are assumed to have wished him ill.
To die of a spear-thrust is natural : that is fair play, so
to speak. But to die of an illness is quite another
matter—it is the work of some skulking magician or of
concealed enemies. Hence, in parts of the primitive
world, death-dealers are unceasingly active. The
spell and the spear are always at work ; the one wiping
off the scores of the other. In exceptional cases, a
difference is perceived between a fatal illness caused by
a sorcerer and a fatal illness developed in the natural
order of things ; and in order to discover to which
category a particular illness belongs, recourse is had to
a post-mortem examination.

To kill a man stealthily by magic is far worse than to
kill him openly with a weapon. He may be able to turn
aside your weapon, but is almost powerless against your
magic, if you knew how to work it properly. So that the
ill-wisher is more dreaded and detested than the ordinary
homicide.

The man who slays openly, however, and thus lets
loose a ghost, usually incurs a penalty of some kind. If

he kills a stranger, people are less likely to be hard on him than if he kills one of his own clan ; and this is almost invariably the case if the stranger is killed on his own territory—a feat which proves real manliness and courage. The ghost has little power outside his tribal boundaries. That is why a war-party, returning from a day's work, hasten to get on their own ground before nightfall. A man-slayer is mystically polluted, and carries with him a spiritual danger which is highly contagious, and may be passed on to the innocent. He is not allowed to touch food with his hands, all the refuse that he leaves must be carefully destroyed, and anyone who incautiously touches his sleeping-rug, or his other belongings, may be placed under the same restrictions as the murderer. A homicide in the Andamans, for example, is pushed out into the jungle, and there he has to stay, waited on by his wife and a friend or two, it may be for some months. Moreover, he has to put red paint on his neck and upper lip and to wear plumes of shredded wood. After the period of seclusion, he is ceremonially purified, but the plumes are worn for a year or so. In various parts of the world, paint and plumes are worn as a disguise, so that the angry ghost may not recognise the slayer.

The attitude taken up by the spirit of a murdered man is not always the same. In Greek mythology, the ghost of a man killed by guile was more to be dreaded than the ghost of one honourably butchered in the wars. That is a distinction which is commonly observed. It is the raging spirit of one treacherously slain, wild for vengeance, which inspires particular terror. So great was the fear of such a spirit among the Eskimo that they used to cut up the body of a murdered person, so that the ghost might be similarly dismembered and helpless ; Rasmussen tells us of a case in which the eyes were cut out of the severed head. An Eskimo child may be killed by the mother, and buried with her murdered husband, so that the little ghost may become the instrument of revenge. Yet, among certain primitives, the soul of one basely murdered may do little more than inflict some trifling hurt on the murderer.

From the point of view of the ghost, there are often serious disadvantages in having been murdered—notably, the trouble of finding an avenger, and of drawing attention to the crime. In this, however, the discarnate soul is sometimes assisted by the body, which bleeds or moves at the approach or touch of the murderer. The criminal may also be detected through the strange behaviour of inanimate things, and by signs and omens. Revenge is a motive commonly attributed to the spirit of a slain person ; and that spirit is assumed to be restless, dangerous, and of a horrible aspect, until appeased by the slaying of some other person—not necessarily the assassin. In places where the angry dead are feared, the atoning murder is committed without loss of time : a life for a life is the primitive law, and a law not so much enforced for the protection of the community from man-slayers as for the protection of the community from bloodthirsty ghosts. As I have said, the ghost does not always make the supreme exaction ; he may content himself by playing some *mauvais tour* on the offender, or by merely disturbing people in a casual way. It depends, of course, on the value of human life in his tribe. In many cases, a fine, or some other form of compensation, appeases the relatives, calms the ghost, and satisfies the conscience of the community. But the fact remains, that a slain man enters upon his ghostly life with a more or less definite resolve to retaliate upon the living. When the Maya Indians had sentenced a man to death, his guards fell upon him while he was asleep, and they all chopped at him together, in order that no one person could be held answerable for the death.

The suicide, whatever his alleged motives, has always

been regarded as a problem. Faith in immortality and
in the unbounded power and freedom of the spirit after
death has sometimes led men to take their own lives
or to submit readily to death at the hands of others.
Posidonius affirms that the Gauls willingly had their
throats cut in the theatre, a spectacle for debauched
Romans, in return for wine or money which was handed
to their friends. Voluntary death as a means toward
the avenging of an affront or injury is no uncommon
thing ; it may, indeed, be inflicted through mere malice
or a love of mischief. But the attitude towards the
suicide varies. He may be feared or he may be utterly
despised. He is despised if there is no clear motive for
his action. He is feared if he is suspected of having
sought freedom for the accomplishment of some mischievous design. Speaking of the Banyankole, a small
Central African tribe, Roscoe tells us " A suicide for
whose deed no reason could be found was buried in
waste land, but if a man or woman committed suicide
for grief at the death of a relative they were buried
with much honour." Concerning the status of the
suicide in the next world there is diversity of opinion :
as he has not approached by the ordinary road, but has
taken a short cut, it is sometimes thought that the rulers
of the spirit-land look on him with disfavour.

We have now learnt something about primitive ideas
in regard to the nature and fate of the soul—ideas which,
in one form or another, are present in the minds of the
greater part of mankind, civilised or uncivilised. We
shall be able to pass on to our examination of burial
rites and the cult of the dead with some knowledge of
their meaning, and with an appreciation of the beliefs
which have dictated their form and controlled their
development.

CHAPTER II

THE CULT OF THE DEAD

Body and soul—Burial, ceremonial, and the cult of the dead—
The technique of burial—The intrinsic properties of the skull
and of the bones—The tomb and its furniture—Ancestor-
worship and the evolution of gods—Mourning.

BODY AND SOUL

ALTHOUGH the spiritual part of a man is conceived of, in primitive thought, as an element
of personality which can exist apart from the
body in which it resides during the earthly life, the connection between soul and body is believed to be more
than a mere sympathetic attachment. Not only does
the ghost linger in the neighbourhood of the body for
many days after death, but the body itself is mysteriously
identified with some continuing aspect of the individual,
with the ghost, or with some new assemblage of the
personal elements for which we have no exact word or
expression. This mysterious aspect of the body applies
also to its separate parts, and even to the products of
decomposition. Primitive man imagines that there are
properties resident in the fat, the blood, the flesh, the
bones of a dead person—properties which are so intimately related to the personality that we can only
describe them as spiritual. A skull, even a jawbone,
even some isolated fragment of a human organism has
an indwelling power or virtue ; it is able to exert influences or to react in accordance with the desires or
circumstances of living persons in a way which proves
that the material of the body and the essence of the soul
are closely, if not inseparably, connected.

33

The primitive notions concerning the bond which unites the soul and the body, even after death, though seemingly illogical and inconsistent, are held with firm conviction. For example, the treatment accorded to the dead body is believed to react in a very definite way on the liberated spirit. When Clytæmnestra mutilated Agamemnon, she did so in order that his angry ghost might be similarly mutilated, and thus hindered from taking revenge. Such procedure is of frequent occurrence among primitive folk. If the head is lopped off, or if the body is bound or broken, or weighted with stones, it is believed that the ghost is likewise maimed or restricted. You may not be able to destroy a ghost, but you may bring it to such a pass that, although living, it is blind and powerless. So, after the man is dead, his toes and thumbs may be tied together, his eyes pierced, his neck pushed under a rock, his carcase buried deep, and a great boulder rolled over the mouth of his sepulchre. Yet all the time it is known that his spirit is not in the tomb : it is roaming about and, it may be, observing all that goes on. In this, there is an apparent confusion. The soul has gone away from the body once for all ; and still, if you injure the body, you injure the soul. But, perhaps, in maiming or binding the body, you are only injuring or restricting the ghost under its human aspect—you are only depriving it of its power to intervene in the domain of purely human activities. If you sever the hands of a dead man, you may be assured that his ghost has no hands wherewith to throttle you in the darkness. Indeed, it is not improbable that one of the purposes of cremation may have been the complete destruction of the human aspect of the ghost or its transference to a region from which contact with mankind, in any material sense, was impossible. (W. de Graft, quoted by Beecham, states that the bones of the ancient dead in Ashanti were dug up and burnt, so as to destroy the spirits, who might otherwise harm the living.) However that may be, it is clear that the conduct and powers of a discarnate human spirit are modified by the treatment of the body in which it formerly lived.

The idea of the multiple soul, of course, solves the difficulty. There is a body-soul and there is a spirit-soul; the former alone being associated with its human relics. But the belief in a multiple soul is not always present to explain matters, and we are left to conclude that, in so far as we are concerned with the mystic relation between the bodily part and the spiritual part of man, we are dealing with a form of primitive thought which, in our present state of knowledge and sophistication, we are unable to subject to a close analysis.

There is another aspect of the union of bodily and spiritual elements; and that is found in the supposed transference of personal qualities through the eating, sacramental or otherwise, of the body, or through the anointing of the living with the fatty or liquescent portions of the body, or through mere contact with the flesh or bones. And the definite association of the surviving personality with some carefully preserved part of the body (the mummified carcase, the head or skull, or the long bones) shows us yet another aspect of the same idea. How it originated we cannot say. A dead body, even the effigy of a body, even something which is suggestive of the human form, the crudest idol, the most capricious or fantastic simulation, a natural freak, conveys an idea of living personality—so deep-rooted is man's essential anthropomorphism. We have a tendency to extend our likeness to all that we see, to imagine faces and forms everywhere, and to endow things neither human nor animate with humanity and animation. Everyone knows the extraordinary suggestiveness of a human skull. Everyone knows how animals with practically no facial mobility are credited by their human lovers with an absolutely human degree of expressiveness. Small wonder that, to primitive man, the body after death nearly always becomes an object which excites the strangest and most powerful emotions.

Only in very exceptional cases (as among certain tribes of the Masai and Wanyamwezi groups in Africa) the body receives no ceremonial treatment, but is abandoned, or thrown on to waste ground, or left on the field of battle. Nevill has said of the Veddas : " The flesh, when the spirit has left it, receives neither veneration nor superstitious reverence. Where the life left the body, there the body was left. . . ." And Seligmann adds : " In any event it is certain that the Veddas did return to caves in which a death had occurred, and that if any bones were left, no difficulty was made about picking these up and casting them into the jungle."

BURIAL, CEREMONIAL, AND THE CULT OF THE DEAD

We of Western Europe, who usually entrust the burial of our dead to a tradesman and the care of their tombs to a jobbing gardener, may find it difficult to realise the significance of the ancient or primitive attitude. Once a man is dead, no matter how dear or valuable to us, the manifold cares and concerns of our civilised life soon drive the very thought of him into the dim background of memory. A burial place is the ugliest and most avoided of localities. But with an uncivilised people, the case is entirely different. Nothing is more real to them than the continued and powerful presence of the dead ; nothing more exacting than the demands made on the world of the living by the world of departed spirits ; nothing more frequently in their minds, and before their eyes, than the affairs of the tomb. Generally speaking, departed ancestors make incessant demands on the time and energy of the " savage," and their concerns occupy a very considerable part of his life. Death, far from being the end of the individual, is the beginning of the individual in his most formidable aspect. In order to understand the cults and the customs which we are about to examine, it is essential that these facts should be remembered. The ceremonials and burial rites of uncivilised man are the expression of what is, to him, the unquestionable and proven truth, that the souls of men are immortal. On this point, the primitive mind, hazy and hesitating as it may be on other matters, is insistently clear.

It cannot be affirmed, as we have already seen, that the primary cult of the dead is based on affection. To the primitive thinker, one loved in life may be terrible in death, a peaceable man may become the most importunate of bullies. The idea of happy reunion with departed friends does not often occur, and this is mainly due to the supposed attitude of the departed themselves. But the cult of the immortal dead, growing out of the ancient belief in survival, appears to be the origin and starting-point of all man's religious and mystic ideas : from the worship of ancestral ghosts he has evolved his gods, and with gods and ghosts has peopled his heavens and hells and his wide realms of fantasy.

Burial is a term somewhat loosely applied to any method of disposing of the dead body, and in default of a better or more familiar word it is here used in that sense. Primitive men bury their dead in an astonishing variety of ways. Apart from the simpler forms of earth-burial, the body may be placed in a tree, sunk in shoal-water, entirely or partly burnt, rammed into a jar, roasted and eaten, pounded to a pulp, cut up into pieces, made to sit or stand or lie on the surface of the ground, or placed on a scaffold ; or it may be subjected to several different processes in succession, and various parts of it treated in a particular manner. Very frequently the flesh is scraped away or rubbed off the bones, or the progress of decomposition is hastened by various means, and the bones then become the special objects of cult or ritual.

THE TECHNIQUE OF BURIAL
CONTRACTED BURIALS

There is one very singular practice which occurs, or has occurred with great frequency, both among prehistoric and primitive races in every part of the world, and that is the practice of burying or burning the body in a particular posture known as the " contracted position." In its typical form, this position is obtained by bending the thighs inward against the trunk, so that knees and chin meet, and by flexing the arms at the elbows in such a way that the hands are brought up to the head or face. Thus, the carcase has the appearance of crouching or squatting ; but it is usually laid on its side in the tomb. In order to maintain this position, body and limbs are tightly swathed in wrappings or bound with cords.

That such a procedure is adopted in every instance as a means of getting the body into a small space is an explanation which cannot be accepted, as we shall see when we examine the burial rites of living primitive races ; and we shall probably be right in ascribing it to one or the other of two opposed intentions—the desire to make the ghost comfortable, or the desire to restrain it. The attitude is either that of a person who is snugly asleep, or of one who is bound and pinioned. I do not think it at all likely that the attitude is intended to simulate the pre-natal position ; although this opinion has been advanced by many writers.

It will be interesting to investigate somewhat closely a practice which is so widely diffused, so consistent in form, and which evidently expresses some thought which has occurred spontaneously to the primitive mind in all ages and among all peoples.

One of the most ancient of all known human burials, that of the Stone Age man of La Chapelle in the Corréze, which is probably not less than 30,000 years old, showed that, although the body lay on its back, the lower limbs had been bent across to the right. Flexed or contracted burials are frequent in later palæolithic times (that of the Chancelade man shows the contracted position in its most violent form), and abundant during the neolithic period, wherever the traces of that period have been discovered. But procedure was not uniform : in the same neolithic cemetery you will find that some of the bodies are curled up while others are straight. It is interesting to note that the Egyptians of the end of the neolithic period buried the sun-dried body sitting in a hole, and that the more usual form of the contracted burial—lying on the side—superseded this practice at a later date.

The custom of bending the body continued throughout the Bronze Age ; and it is observable that bodies were burnt in that position, and that the bodies of children were treated in precisely the same way as those of adults. The detailed examination of prehistoric burials is reserved for another chapter ; here we merely note the extreme antiquity of this peculiar manner of disposing of the body.

In Africa, the Bongo people force the knees of a corpse up to its chin, bind it round the head and legs, and sew it up in a skin sack. The Bahima resort to violent measures, and the arms and legs are doubled up with broken joints ; the neck is also broken, and the head forced down onto the thorax. Among the Lendu, the body of a chief is bound in a sitting posture with strips of bark-cloth. The Kikuyu folk only bury persons of a certain standing ; the knees are doubled up, and the right hand placed under the head. One of the Bantu tribes in South-East Africa sets the body in the desired position before it is dead, forcing the thighs against the abdomen and the arms against the trunk, and binding them tightly ; and Roscoe, speaking of the Bakonjo, a people of the Uganda Protectorate, tells us " When

death occurred, the first step was to place the body in
the correct position for burial, and in many cases the
attendants did not wait until the man was actually
dead to do this. When they saw that he was dying,
they would bend up his legs and cross his arms in front
of him so that he might die in that position." Other
African folk prepare the body in this manner immediately
the breath has left it, if not before. The king of the
Banyankole was made ready for burial by having his
legs bent up, his right arm was placed under his head
and his left arm on his breast. The king of the Bakitara
was buried with his knees under his chin, and both his
hands under the right side of his head, the entire body
closely swathed in white bark-cloths. The body of
a Bakitara queen was also placed in the squatting
posture.

In South-East Australia, the Narrang-ga, after carrying the corpse about for several weeks on a sort of round
bier, bury it with the knees doubled up close to the
face. The Tongaranka bury their dead sitting. Among
the Wotjobaluk people a man was buried curled up like
a bale, with his knees on his chest and his arms crossed ;
and in the Mukjarawaint clan, the knees were drawn up,
the elbows brought to the sides and the hands to the
shoulders. The Ngarigo used to bury with the knees
touching the head, and the hands on either side of the
face (Howitt).

The New Caledonians place the dead in a crouching
attitude, with the head near, or even above, the surface
of the ground, so that there is no difficulty in removing
the skull Of the Hervey Islanders we are told that
" If a body were buried in the earth, it was always laid
face downwards, with chin and knees meeting, and the
limbs well secured with coco-nut fibre " (Frazer). In
the typical burial of the Society Islanders, the arms
are bound to the shoulders, the legs bent under the
thighs and forced against the stomach : the hands are

sometimes tied to the knees or legs. The Hawaiians give a somewhat unusual example : the bodies of the common folk were buried in the crouching posture, with the face bent towards the knees and the hands passed under the thighs and brought inside the knees, all tightly corded together ; but the bodies of important people were laid out straight. According to W. H. R. Rivers, one of the most gifted and observant of anthropologists, the Solomon Islanders, among their diverse forms of burial, occasionally set the corpse in a sitting position with the limbs tightly bound ; and he says that there is definite evidence from Mangaia that this binding was intended " to prevent the return of the dead man." Rivers makes this comment : " If interment in the contracted position is believed to prevent the return of the deceased, it is evident that we have in it the manifestation of ideas radically opposed to those connected with preservation of the body among the living." This case, in which an explanation of the motives responsible for the contracted form of burial has been actually given by the people who practise it, is of remarkable interest.

The Jesuit, Pierre Biard, writing more than three centuries ago, thus described the burial technique of the Mississippi Indians : " They swathe the body and tie it up in skins . . . with the knees against the stomach and the head on the knees, as we are in our mother's womb." Flexed burial was in vogue among the Indians long after the arrival of the settlers, and in New England such a burial has been found accompanied by brass objects of European manufacture. But the Indian cemeteries, like those of the neolithic men in Europe, contain both flexed and straight interments. The Hurons usually contracted the body. In Yucatan, the Maya Indians practised both methods : they employed occasionally an extraordinarily violent form of contraction, setting the body upside down with the skull in a prepared cavity and the neck jammed under a block of stone, while the knees touched the rock on either side of the head. A case of extreme contraction was found in one of their burial mounds : the legs and thighs were forced up, and the curvature of the back brought the head almost within the pelvic basin.

Among the Andaman Islanders, the body, after the head had been shaved and the whole carcase bedaubed with paint and pipeclay, was buried with the knees drawn up under the chin and the clenched hands pressed into the cheeks.

The Tasmanian aborigines made use of the flexed position, for we are told by Robinson that, after a man had died they " bent the legs back against the thighs, and bound them together with twisted grass. Each arm was bent together, and bound round above the elbow "— and the body was then burnt.

Here, then, is a burial usage which is of world-wide distribution and of incredibly ancient origin. What is the meaning of it ? In one case we appear to have the explanation of a people practising the rite, and they say that it is done in order to restrain the dead man, to arrange him in such a way that he cannot rush out of the tomb and become a terror to his former comrades. That is a very likely explanation, but it is possible that it does not apply to every case. Where the flexion of the limbs is not violent, as in many neolithic graves in Europe and in the earliest dynastic burials in Egypt, and in similar forms of burial among living races, it may very well be that the attitude is intended to simulate that of comfortable sleep. It is just conceivable that the idea of economising space may account for exceptional instances : it is not valid as a general explanation, because a single contracted burial may occupy only one corner of a large and completed tomb, and because the bodies of kings and chieftains are treated in this way. We are probably right in assuming that, in the great majority of cases, restraint is the predominant motive. Owing to the singular confusion of primitive thought which we have spoken of above, it is assumed that whatever happens to the dead body happens also to the ghost ; but apart from this, it is not unlikely that the body itself, re-animated by the spirit, might be supposed to force its way from the sepulchre if it were not prevented from doing so by drastic measures.

THE ASSOCIATION OF RED COLOUR WITH BURIALS

There is another strange detail of burial technique, common both to prehistoric man and to his living representatives, and that is the application of red colour to the bodies or bones of the dead, and its general association with funeral affairs. Whether the colour is applied merely as a decoration, or whether it has a symbolic meaning, is a question that we shall be in a better position to answer if we examine a few instances of the practice.

Morsels of red ochre have been found in graves of the middle palæolithic period, although there is no instance of coloured bones which can be ascribed to that date. But from the beginning of the upper palæolithic period (the Aurignacian stage) coloration is much in evidence. Sometimes a paste of red ochre seems to have been rubbed over the entire body ; sometimes it would appear that the colour has been applied to the desiccated bones ; and in other cases, the body has been laid in a couch of ochreous earth. Thus, in seeking for the origin of this custom, we have to go back some 20,000 years at least.

In the neolithic phase, the practice is strongly marked, and it is often accompanied by the provision of supplies of red colouring matter, either in pinches or morsels placed in grooves in the earth or in the hand of the deceased, or in little pots. Moreover, the objects found within the grave are occasionally stained red. There can be little doubt that the supplies of ochre were cosmetics, meant for the use of the departed : they may be regarded as the equivalents of the rouge and lipsticks of to-day. With the coming of the metal ages, this particular practice, in Europe, begins to die out.

Let us now see in what form this usage appears among people of recent or of modern times.

One of the Pilgrim Fathers wrote the following account of the contents of an Indian burial mound : Upon opening the mound, they discovered, he says, " first a Matt, and under that a fayre Bow, and there another Matt, and under that boord about three-quarters long, finely carved and paynted . . . also between the Matts we found Boules, Trayes, Dishes, and such like Trinkets : at length we came to a fayre new Matt, and under that two Bundles, the one bigger, the other less, we opened the greater and found in it a great quantitie of fine and perfect red Powder, and in it the bones and skull of a man . . . a knife, a pack-needle, and two or three old iron things. It was bound up in a Sayler's canvas Cassack and a payre of cloth breeches. . . . We opened the less bundle likewise, and found of the same Powder in it, and the bones and head of a little childe "—within this bundle were also some strings of white beads and a little bow, with " some other odd knacks." The " fine and perfect red Powder " was probably red oxide of iron, which has been found in many similar burials : the provision of red oxide was, in fact, an established custom of the Algonquian tribes who occupied the coast of New England. In 1762 the burial of the wife of a great Delaware chief was witnessed by a European, who tells us that her body, richly dressed and bedecked, was painted with vermilion (red mercuric sulphide), and that a small bag of vermilion paint, together with some flannel for applying it, was pushed in through a hole at the head of the coffin. The Choctaw decorated the skulls of their dead with a preparation of bear's oil and vermilion.

According to Lawson (1701) the Monacan Indians used to expose corpses to the action of the sun, after which they treated them with " a small root beaten to powder, which looks as red as vermilion." After the decay of the flesh, the bones were coloured with the same red powder mixed with oil, and carefully preserved in a wooden box, to be cleaned, oiled, and coloured every year. The Pascagoulas dried and smoked the body of a chief, painted it red, and tied it upright to a long pole.

The funeral use of red is frequent in Africa. The Niam–Niam (a cannibal people) adorned the dead body with skins and feathers and dyed it with red wood. In the Congo the corpse is dried over a slow fire, and then plastered from head to foot with red clay, or reddened by being rubbed all over with oil and powdered camwood. The Ndolo covered the body with a paste made from red bark. Beecham (1841) relates how the Fanti people used to bedeck the dead man in all his finery and lay him out on a sofa, under a silk umbrella, in a room entirely hung with red cloth. He mentions women at the funeral rites in Ashanti " daubed with red earth, in barbarous imitation of those who had succeeded in besmearing themselves with the blood of the victims." Whether he is right or not in considering this a " barbarous imitation," the idea of the use of red as symbolic of blood is worth taking into account. Modern Africans continue the ancient custom, and still colour their dead with camwood powder and fat, with greasy preparations of iron oxide, or with oil and red earth.

The native Australians do not furnish many examples of this practice, but the Narrinyeri applied grease and red ochre to the body, before drying it over a fire ; and the Gnanji stained the arm bones with red ochre for magical purposes. In all the Maori forms of burial, the bones were ultimately removed, scraped and cleaned, and usually painted red. Darwin has described the funeral of a New Zealand princess, and he says that " her body being enclosed between two small canoes, was placed upright on the ground, and protected by an enclosure bearing wooden images of their gods, and the whole was painted bright red."

In the Torres Straits Islands, the head of a dead man was sawn off his body, picked clean in an ant-heap painted red, and placed in an elegant basket : entire bodies were sometimes dried, and then coloured. The Yabim of New Guinea adorn the skulls and long bones of their eminent men with red paint, and preserve them reverently ; and a similar practice is observed in the case of the Tami.

A dead Andaman Islander is decorated by being streaked with alternate bands of white clay and red paint, with a line of red paint drawn from ear to ear across the upper lip ; and in due course his exhumed skull and jawbone are treated in similar fashion.

Thus we see that the finest and fiercest of colours has been associated throughout the world with the rites of the tomb. The Sphinx, in all probability one of the hugest and most impressive of funerary monuments, fit emblem of the riddle of death, had a red face. What is the significance of this association ? Macalister, in his *Text Book of European Archæology*, says, " The purpose of the rite [dyeing the bodies and bones of the deceased] is perfectly clear. Red is the colour of living health." I do not agree with him. Even from the limited selection of examples which we have passed in review we may safely draw the conclusion that the purpose of the rite is not always the same, and that in some cases it is far from being " perfectly clear." It is natural enough to suppose that the dead man should wish to enter the halls of death in all his finery, and that the application of red to his face or person would help him to present a gracious and striking appearance. In the case of the Delaware burial, the dead lady was actually supplied with a bit of flannel in order that she might be able to rouge herself. A similar explanation—the desire to enhance the personal appearance of the ghost— is available for a great number of instances, both pre-historic and modern, and it is an essentially reasonable explanation. Again, red is not the " colour of living health " to a swarthy or black-skinned people ; and in their case, if we look for symbolism at all, we must look for symbolism of another kind. If it is correct, that the women mourners of Ashanti coloured their bodies red in order to simulate anointment with sacrificial blood, the same idea of blood-symbolism might very well be applied to the corpse. But we are too ready to attach a mystic meaning to the simple acts of primitive man. Sooner than advocate an explanation which is based on some obscurely conceived idea of magic or symbolism, I would submit that the practice of reddening the dead body, the skull or the bones, in all instances where its meaning may be regarded as clear, is a practice having for its sole aim the achievement of splendour or comeli-ness ; that it represents the continuance beyond the grave of a custom which has been steadily in use among the living—a custom so natural and so simple that it seems foolish to look for other motives. As for the paint-ing of the selected bones which are preserved for the purpose of cult, that is probably done in order to make them attractive. Red is naturally chosen, because it is the most easily obtained and most resplendent colour which nature offers ; and also, perhaps, because it promotes ideas of warmth, cheerfulness, and vitality.

CANNIBALISM AND SACRIFICE

Promiscuous anthropophagy—the eating of men as mere food, on account of the succulence of their flesh— is different altogether from the eating of a dead body with the idea of obtaining spiritual nourishment, and of absorbing sacramentally the virtues of the deceased. The eating of human flesh for purely gastronomic reasons (apart from recourse to this dreadful diet in times of food-shortage) is a rare and revolting practice. Human meat was at one time publicly offered for sale in parts of Africa, and not more difficult to obtain there than venison is here ; but that is not the case at the present day. As for the eating of dead bodies, whether of friends or foes, and the use of their fat or other products as lotions and embrocations—these are customs which occur so infrequently that we cannot deal with them in a general way : we shall reserve description of them until Chapter IV, when we shall make a more extended and detailed examination of primitive burial rites. It should be noted, that the devouring of a corpse as part of the funeral rites, or for a definitely spiritual reason, is not cannibalism in the popular sense of the word. In some cases, indeed, the eating consists only of pantomime, and even if the flesh is placed in the mouth, it is hastily spat out again.

Corpses, it is true, may be eaten in the ordinary cannibalistic sense—as they were by the Fan, who lived on the west coast of Equatorial Africa, and who not only bartered the bodies of their dead among themselves, but actually dug up corpses in order to devour them. But there is hardly another instance of such ghoulish gluttony.

Human sacrifice is a fairly ordinary accompaniment of primitive burial in its more highly evolved forms. The reasons for funerary sacrifice are : (a) the providing of the dead ruler with a retinue, with affectionate consorts, with slaves and messengers ; (b) the desire to strengthen the shade of the deceased with the fat and blood of the victims, so that he may be burly and boastful in the world of spirits, as he was during his carnal existence ; (c) the mere dread of the ghost, who will not cease to haunt and harry the survivors if he is not given his dues. There are also political reasons, such as the rooting up of an unpopular dynasty or the removal of tyrannous administrators. Sacrifice is graded in accordance with rank and with local custom. There may be only one victim (a wife, or favourite concubine), there may be some dozens, some hundreds, or even two or three thousand. Sacrifice may be repeated at each anniversary of the death, or at stated times of commemoration. It was in Africa that sacrifice grew to a monstrous horror, and the grave of a king was a pit full of blood and abomination. In Dahomey, only kings were buried with human vicitims, and the number of those slain to accompany them is alleged to have totalled two thousand, or more, at a single funeral. Beecham (who must be suspected, however, of being an ardent propagandist) says that one of the kings of Ashanti killed four thousand human victims on the occasion of his brother's departure for ghost-land. Prehistoric graves afford evidence of human immolation, very frequently of women and children, but not in considerable numbers. The evidence often shows that the victims of the sacrifice were of a different build and race from the person whose ghost they were intended to serve, and the inference is that they were slaves or prisoners of war.

The carcases of animals are placed with those of men either (*a*) as mere property, (*b*) as food, (*c*) as offerings to the gods of the underworld, (*d*) as being of service to the ghost—e.g., the horses buried with the chariot of the ancient Keltic warrior. An animal may be slain on the occasion of a death in order that its life may cheer and fortify the spirit of the dead man. Thus, the animal victim becomes a substitute for the human victim. We shall see that animal bones, mingled with the bones of men, are almost invariably found in certain types of prehistoric burial.

CREMATION

In 1892, the United States Cremation Company employed the ingenious Mr. Cobb to write a book for them. Mr. Cobb dilated, with brilliance and in a harrowing manner, on the horrors of interment and the advantages of burning. You would have thought that no one, after reading his gloomy and powerful book, could have been in doubt for one single second. Yet the fact remains, that cremation has had but a mediocre success in the States, as elsewhere.

Cremation has never had more than a mediocre success, except during certain phases of the prehistoric and protohistoric ages. At no time, and among no people, has it been universally adopted. In spite of, perhaps because of, the fear of the ghost, the idea of destroying a dead body by fire has never found lasting favour. On no other point of usage have men been so resolutely conservative.

The primitive motives for cremation are, (a) the desire to achieve a compact form of personal burial, (b) regard for convenience in transport, (c) the complete liberation of the spirit, (d) the rapid disposal of a body, when there is no time for orthodox burial, (e) social distinction— though curiously enough, to be burnt is sometimes a mark of honour and sometimes the reverse. Perhaps one might append, as suggesting yet another motive, the following observation from *Hydriotaphia* : " To be gnawed out of our graves, to have our skulls made drinking bowls, and our bones turned into pipes, to delight and sport our enemies, are tragical abominations escaped in burning burials." A corpse is looked on as a thing so holy, and so dangerous to those who show it disrespect, that the majority of mankind has submitted to the most repulsive and troublesome of expedients, sooner than consign the dead to the clean and nobly symbolic action of fire. It is difficult to see what can be urged against the practice of burning the dead, either on religious or practical grounds ; easy to see what can be urged in its favour ; but the truth is, that the old affection for the body, even the decaying and loathsome body, has always persisted, always triumphed, and is still persistent and triumphant to-day.

In the primitive practice of cremation, there is no uniform method ; on the contrary, there is a great variety of method, and the action of the fire may be limited to a mere scorching or broiling or extended to complete incineration. Parts of the body may be reserved for burning, and parts disposed of in some other manner. Neither is there any uniformity in the treatment of the ashes.

Burning the corpse is seldom, if ever, the invariable custom among any one people, though it appears to be so nowadays in the case of the Todas. It is also very widely if not universally adopted by the Arawak Indians of South Guiana and Northern Brazil. The most primitive of observed instances of cremation occurred among the Tasmanians—folk who were living in a stage of culture not more advanced than that of the early palæolithic races of Europe. But our records of Tasmanian life are unreliable, and we cannot say whether such cases occurred frequently ; apparently they did not. In Europe, no prehistoric graves afford absolute proof of cremation before the concluding phases of the neolithic age. There is no reason, however, for supposing that the burning of the dead was unknown in palæolithic times.

ORIENTATION

At all periods, and among different races, we find a tendency, by no means invariable, to place the inhumed body in some definite relation to the points of the compass. Such procedure gives further proof of a belief in the close connection between body and soul, or in some form of consciousness which is never separated from the body.

Although far from constant, the usual disposition of an oriented body is to arrange it so that the face looks towards the rising sun. The Andaman people believe that the sun would be prevented from rising if this orientation were not observed. In tombs of the Third Egyptian Dynasty at Reqâqnah, the vaulted chambers contained bodies which were in every case facing due east. Similar orientation is frequent in modern Africa : the body of the Hottentot, sewn up in blood-soaked wrappings, sits with face towards the dawn. And though no ray of light can reach the perfect darkness and stillness of the tomb, this peculiar sympathy between the dead body and the sun is probably the reason for every instance of systematic orientation.

The predynastic cemetery at El Mahasna contained bodies lying on the left side, in the contracted posture, with the head to the south. In this case, the faces were turned towards the setting, not the rising, sun. Of prehistoric burials in general, it may be observed that orientation is not constant, though there is often a marked preference for setting the body on a line between east and west. The eastern end of the neolithic burial mound in Europe, like the eastern side of the Egyptian mastaba, is of particular importance and sanctity. An exception may be cited from the Iron Age cemetery of Jeserine in Bosnia, where the greater number of the burials, which were laid out straight, were placed on a north-south alignment, with the head to the north. Keltic interments of the La Tène period are usually extended on an east-west alignment, with the head to the west ; but in the great tumulus of Lantilly, the sixty-five burials were placed in a seemingly random fashion. Canon Greenwell, who was a field archæologist of the first order, speaking of the prehistoric burials on the Yorkshire Wolds excavated by him, said that " There is no rule as regards the direction of the body, the head being laid with the face opposite to any point of the compass." Thus, it is clear that orientation has never been a constant factor in the burial rites of ancient or primitive people, though, when it does occur, it tends to show a similarity of intention and to establish an imagined relation between the position of the dead body and the course of the sun. Our Christian cemeteries give us, in this respect, one of the numerous instances which the study of comparative religion so freely affords, of the retention of a pagan ritual.

THE INTRINSIC PROPERTIES OF THE SKULL AND OF THE BONES

In view of the assumed close connection between the body and the spirit, and the frequent identification of the one with the other, it is natural enough that the dead body, or any portion of it, should be supposed to contain peculiar powers and virtues. Human relics are treasured equally by the pious Christian and by the untaught savage ; and it may be that there is little to choose between the power of a saint's bones and those of a Melanesian chief. The sentiment in regard to human remains is strongly operative, even in the case of civilised or irreligious people, and there are few who can look on human bones with cold indifference. (Primitive folk often make a distinction, in this respect, between the remains of their own kinsmen and those of strangers. For example, Schweinfurth tells us that the Monbuttu brought him an immense number of skulls and jawbones, but these were nearly all relics of the members of other tribes who had been eaten ; and the skulls had for the most part been smashed to facilitate the removal of the brains. Such distinction is not peculiar to the uncivilised, as many of us learnt in the Great War.)

The head or skull is regarded as something which is intensely personal and powerful. Indeed, the possession of a man's head is sometimes considered as the means of holding his spirit in a state of thraldom. The head-hunter believes that his trophies ensure a supply of ghostly servitors, both here and in the life hereafter.

That is a belief common to the Kelt of early historic times and to the Dyak of Borneo. Drinking from a skull transferred the vitality of its original owner to those who drank : a draught of milk from the skull of Conall Cernach gave courage to the faint-hearted and feeble ; and it was believed in the Scotch Highlands that a drink from the skull of a suicide was efficacious in restoring health.

The cult of ancestral skulls is frequently encountered, and it still prevails, under a pseudo-religious guise, in many parts of Europe. It was formerly the custom in Brittany, on All Saint's Eve, for priest and people to walk to the charnel houses, where the parochial skulls, neatly placed in black, white, and blue boxes, with heart-shaped openings, grinned a welcome to the visitors. In certain chapels and mortuary shrines in the Austrian Tyrol, rows of skulls, sometimes painted and labelled, bear witness to the cult, and most travellers in the less known parts of Europe are aware of similar instances.

It is among the islanders of the great ocean that we find the full development of the skull-cult. W. H. R. Rivers has written : " The prominent feature of the existing cult of the dead in the Solomons is the importance of the skull. In these islands . . . the whole religious ritual centres round the skulls of ancestors and relatives, which are long preserved in special shrines and are the object of numerous rites." He thinks this is due to the idea that the head is " the symbol or representative of a person." Even in cases where the majority of the bones are buried or sunk, the skull is retained. That is sometimes annoying to the ghost. Thus, in the Torres Straits Islands, the party carrying the recovered skull in its decorated basket, in order to hand it over to the relatives, were met with a flight of arrows (aimed high), so that the gullible ghost might be tricked into the belief that his friends were seriously angry. Skulls are used for divination, and they are the centres of, and chief participators in, the great island festivals.

The personal importance of the skull is shared to some extent by the lower jawbone. In the Hood Peninsula of New Guinea, a widow wears her dead husband's waistband round her head with his jawbone attached to it. The Tamos, in the same island, take the lower jaw from the burial place, some months after the interment, with great ceremony ; and the Kai appear to bury all the bones with the exception of the jawbone. A. R. Brown relates that the Andaman Islanders attributed his illness and that of several natives to the fact that he had a human jawbone hanging in his hut in such a way that it swung in the wind : he was begged to put it in a basket, where it could not move. The lower maxillary is often one of the bones specially chosen to become the centres of cult. Every ethnologist has read of the great Agranhowe umbrella of Dahomey, decorated with no fewer than eighty-four human jawbones, elegantly disposed in a chevron pattern. The Baganda remove the lower jaws of dead kings, and in Uganda the king's jawbone is placed on a wooden dish within a shrine. The Wahuma decorated their royal jawbones with beads. When a Busoga chief was buried, his tomb was provided with a shaft which reached down to the head, and beneath this was a little hollow containing a basket : a bell was attached to the head, and when this rotted off from the body and fell into the basket, the guardians of the tomb, duly advised by the ringing of the bell, drew up the basket and removed the jawbone.

The New Caledonians have family skull stores, where the ancestral relics are preserved and venerated, and prayed to in times of trouble. Throughout Oceania the cult of skulls is of primary importance, and what Rivers has said of the Solomons is applicable to most of the Pacific Islands. In many cases, bits of gleaming shell or cowries are stuck in the eye-sockets, features are crudely modelled in wax, missing teeth are replaced by wooden pegs, and the facial parts are brilliantly painted. The natives of eastern Borneo used to decorate skulls with beautiful and elaborate curvilinear designs. Even the Tasmanian aborigines appear to have known the cult, for West (1829) gives an account of the removal of the skull from a cremated body, and he says that it was " long worn, wrapped in a kangaroo skin " by a woman who was assumed to have been the mother of the deceased.

In Africa, skulls are decorated and preserved, although they have not the same religious meaning that they possess elsewhere. But they have powerful or dangerous qualities. In a Bantu village, people are greatly disturbed if some foolish or wicked person runs about with a skull, and the whole place becomes *thahu*—that is, extremely vulnerable to the attacks of evil spirits. Among the Masai, the skull of a chief is preserved by his eldest son, and it gives him power and wisdom. Skertchly (1874) says that he had a man's skull fixed over the lintel of the door of his quarters at Abomey by a fetiche-doctor, as a protective measure.

Prehistoric burials give evidence, occasionally (as in the mysterious skull-burials at Ofnet, in Bavaria), of what appear to have been rituals in connection with heads or skulls, but we cannot be certain of the intention in such cases.

The other bones of the human skeleton are often treated in a ceremonial or superstitious manner. The Tumleo people of New Guinea, after digging up the bones of their dead, place the skull and a thigh-bone in the club house, fasten the vertebræ to their bracelets, make necklaces of the ribs, and decorate their baskets with the shoulder-blades. In Rauro or San Cristoval, bones or teeth are hung in a basket from the main post of every house.

A dead hand, or the bones of it, has peculiar powers.

The Kurnai, one of the Victorian tribes of Australia, would sometimes cut the hand from a corpse, wrap it in grass, and dry it carefully : it was then worn by one of the corpse's near relations, tied to a strip of twisted fur, and in contact with the skin under the left arm. At the approach of an enemy, the dead hand would pinch the wearer, who then pulled it up and hung it in front of his face. Another instance of belief in the power of this particular relic may be found in Ireland, where the hand of an unbaptised child, taken from the grave in the name of the devil, is tremendously efficacious in butter-making, burglarious exploit, the curing of disease and the working of charms. And readers of the *Ingoldsby Legends* will remember the grim and splendid lines in the Nurse's Story. It is not strange, perhaps, that belief in the properties of the dead hand should be accepted by the lonely Australian, the Irish wizard, and the Kentish cut-throat, and by many others besides.

The use of bones as charms or amulets may be traced from prehistoric times. Their use for ceremonial purposes, for magical or medical requirements, as tokens of authority, and as the chief " props " of a heathen festival is almost world-wide, and is not by any means peculiar to the uncivilised. As a concluding instance of the part played by human relics in ceremonial, the following is taken from Beecham's book on Ashanti : At the lesser Adai Custom, the bones of the king's mother and sisters were taken our of their coffins, bathed in rum and water, rolled in gold-dust, and wrapped in strings of rock-gold, aggry beads and other costly materials. The king then ordained the slaughter of all the persons of his entourage who were in any way offensive to him, and the graves of the royal women were saturated with the blood of these unfortunates. No one—not the highest official—was safe. By this means, the dead were gratified, and the king, while accomplishing a pious duty, had the satisfaction of removing any courtier or minister who had become a nuisance. Piety and policy were thus happily united ; a union neither so unnatural nor so uncommon as we might think.

THE TOMB AND ITS FURNITURE

Although the fully elaborated tomb belongs to an advanced phase of culture, temporary shelters for the dead or shallow excavations for the reception of their bodies are found at a very early stage of human development. The motive for digging a pit or building a shelter appears identical with that which leads to the construction of all tombs—the desire to provide protection for the body and accommodation for the resident or visiting soul. The wish to remove the body from sight, to dispose of it in such a way that nothing can remind the living of its presence, does not account for primitive burial. Primitive man is quite unaffected by the process of corruption ; the proximity of a rotting corpse causes him neither mental nor physical discomfort. The primitive tomb, therefore, is not a mere receptacle. It is a residence. It is a place where the individual, in his changed aspect, lives with his favourite belongings ; where he is attended and cared for by his friends ; and whence he still exerts his influence on their fears or affections or fancies. No religion of modern times has been able to destroy the ancient belief that the dead haunt their burial places : like the cemetery of the Dyaks, the Christian churchyard is peopled with twilight horrors.

A tomb may be above or below the level of the ground, or partly above and partly below. The upper structure varies from a scarcely perceptible mound to a colossal pyramid.

Together with the body or bodies or the particular human relics which are selected for burial it is customary to place food, weapons, ornaments, and personal attendants, or images representing them, within the tomb. But it does not follow that the whole of the dead man's belongings will be deposited in or near his grave. Custom varies greatly in this respect. It is true that in a vast number of cases the dead take with them their treasured objects, through " vain apprehensions that they might use them in the other world." In other cases a selection is made ; or the property of the deceased is given away to the relatives, or bartered ; or it is ceremonially purified and made harmless, so that the survivors may touch it without fear of death or sickness. Things of special value or rarity may be kept back, and the more ordinary things placed with the corpse. In the Ladrones, the entire property is ruthlessly destroyed. The breaking or spoiling of objects is a common practice ; and sometimes this is done with the idea of " killing " them, so that their ghosts are free to accompany their owner.

As a typical example of what is meant by " grave furniture," I will give the contents of a predynastic Egyptian grave, excavated by Ayrton and Loat at El Mahasna : The body was that of a male, slightly flexed ; he lay in an oblong wood-lined grave, and with him were the following things : near the face, a diorite staff-head, a stone mace-head, two stone picks, a copper harpoon, and two flint flakes ; and close to his head were three pottery vases, an ivory vase, and a clay mace ; there was a broken pot near his knees, and there were also the skeletons of two dogs on their backs, wrapped in a mat, and at their heads were " numerous imitation bunches of garlic in whitened clay."

ANCESTOR-WORSHIP AND THE EVOLUTION OF GODS

Primitive man is so constituted that his reverence grows from his fears, and from his fears alone. It is true that affection is sometimes present in his attitude towards the dead, but this affection is a secondary, almost a fortuitous element. Fear comes first. In all probability the early gods were produced through the development of the cult of the ancestral dead ; and gods, be it noted, are usually feared before they are loved. Indeed, the god and the ancestor are frequently identified (there have been many divine fathers), and it may be said that every primitive god is a resurrection.

The conception of a spirit animating the forms and forces of nature, or residing in them, could not have occurred prior to the concept of " spirit " pure and simple ; and it seems clear that this concept grew out of the belief in human immortality. Man fashions gods in the likeness of his own ghostly double ; he sees in them extended and magnified aspects of the human soul, the human senses, and the human passions.

In order that we may find out in what way the cult of the ancestor originates and develops, we will take some instances, chosen from ancient evidence or primitive practice.

The worship of ancestors is unquestionably the most important element in the native religions of Africa. In some cases, it is the only religious element which appears to be present. It was to the terrible ghosts of their kings, not to full-blown divinities (for they had none), that the Western Sudan negroes offered the dark blood of sacrifice. It is at the ancestor-shrines of their villages that the Bantu negroes slay goats and rams in order to propitiate the shades of their forefathers. Here, and in a great number of similar cases, the ancestor receives what become in more developed cultures the dues of the god—prayers and sacrifice.

According to Du Chaillon, the fear of the dead is found everywhere among the peoples of Equatorial Africa, and the fear is strong until the memory of the departed has grown faint. And as memory grows faint, the more recent dead take the place of the more ancient, and so fear is perpetuated. The Barotse worship the shades of their fathers, and to them, in times of public distress, they make offerings of grain and honey. Sir Wallis Budge, speaking generally of the Bantu people, says, " They appear to have no actual religion, or belief in gods, as apart from ghosts and ancestral influences." Images, representing or containing the ancestral spirits, are characteristic objects in the ghost-cults of modern and of ancient Africa ; and in places these figures are regarded with mistrust and with terror. The African looks upon old men with awe and treats them with punctilious care and with reverence : he knows that the ghost, even while resident in the frail and emaciated body, is taking note of his demeanour, and he knows that any neglect on his part may have tragic results, for him, when the roving soul has him at its mercy. The Kikuyu people believe that the family ghosts live underground ; and the Kamba, that they live in holy fig-trees—and woe betide the man who invades one of the sacred plantations, for he will certainly be pelted by the shadowy tree-dwellers. The Kikuyu head-man offers a ram at his father's grave three or four times each year ; while the Kamba have a sacred place which is common to a group of villages, and there they assemble to pray to the *aiinu* or ancestral ghosts. The Kitui people see the ghosts of their departed friends, and when a Kitui man has observed one of these phantasms, he has to undergo a very nauseating ritual : he has to kill a ram and smear its fat and the contents of its stomach all over his face (Hobley).

Ancestor-worship was nowhere more fully developed and nowhere more bloody in its religious performance than in the kingdoms of Ashanti and Dahomey. Annual ceremonies were held by the kings in honour of their forefathers, and at these ceremonies a prodigious number of human victims was offered to the royal shades. The essentially religious character of the So-sin ritual in Dahomey is clearly shown in the words of Skertchly, who actually witnessed it : " A herald announced that the customs would begin at once, as the king was anxious to prevent his father becoming impatient, but that he wished them to know that he, Gelélé, the lion-king, was still mindful of the ancient customs of his forefathers, and would strive to fulfil all the wishes of his ancestors." And the Sin Kwain ceremonies were even more exclusively centred on the same cult : during those ceremonies, the king visited the ancestral graves, and slept for several nights in each of the palaces of his predecessors ; the ghosts were invoked by " the sacrifice of men and animals, whose blood is sprinkled . . . upon the fetiche-irons which are swathed in calico and guarded in the spirit-houses of each of the kings." At the royal tombs, the king was hailed by the ghost-mothers, women in whom the spirits of the dead monarchs resided, and who spoke, not as messengers from the dead, but as the dead themselves, incarnate and audible. Finally we have the king, in a speech to the populace, declaring that his father after his death had become the greatest of all fetiches, and that the people should therefore pray to him. The royal ghost had acquired the rank and privileges of a god.

The cult of ancestors is fairly general throughout the islands of the Pacific, but the attitude towards the departed seems to differ very considerably. Abject fear alternates with a sense of friendly protection.

The Australian aborigines never evolved a belief in gods, though they revered the memory of their ancestors, whom they credited with unusual wisdom. The ancestors were in some cases prevented from achieving divine status through the fact that they were being continually reborn in their descendants.

Throughout Melanesia, the ghosts of important men receive worship, but they are pushed aside by the succeeding dead, and there are thus no stationary or traditional figures among them, who might reasonably hope to become gods. The Melanesian religion, it would seem, consists of the cult of the recently dead : a sort of " moving shadow show." W. J. Perry informs us that some of the Indonesian folk carry their ancestral spirits about in little pieces of stone, and that similar stones (taken from the graves by old women) are placed in the houses, so that the ghosts may live in them.

In Micronesia we find instances of belief in the friendly nature of the dead. Dealing with the Mortlock Islanders (in the Caroline group) Sir J. G. Frazer says : " Every man believes himself to be compassed about by the souls of his departed forefathers ; they . . . protect him from dangers, and know what will befall him. But they cannot speak with everybody, only with a particular class of persons, the spirit-seers or necromancers "— with " mediums " in fact. The souls of the dead Mortlock chiefs are the gods of the clans ; but it must be admitted that there are many other gods, apart from the deified ancestors. " The national religion of the natives of Yap, according to Father Sixtus Walleser, is fundamentally nothing but the worship of ancestors." But the Yap Islander has no confidence in the good intentions of the dead. He thinks that the souls of his parents, his brothers and sisters and grown-up children, are likely to be mischievous ; and although some spirits may be well disposed and kindly, he is careful to propitiate them all, so as to be on the safe side.

The Pelew Islanders seem to afford an extraordinarily good example of the cult of the dead in its purely and uniquely religious form. They worship the ghosts of kinsfolk, each head of a family acting as priest in his own household. The ghosts are regarded as friendly and protective. " The place in the house which these spirits usually frequent is a sort of cupboard or store-room . . . and it is here that the offerings for the spirits are deposited. If there is no such cupboard in the house, the offerings are placed on one of the cross-beams or on a chest in the corner. These places serve as altars and are devoted to the worship of the domestic and family gods as well as to that of the ancestral spirits" (Frazer). But it is probable that the "domestic and family gods" are only the ancestors (perhaps the remoter ancestors) in another guise. "On Kubary's theory the religion of the Pelew Islanders began and ended with the worship of the dead, after passing through an intermediate stage in the worship of nature, which, according to him, was only the worship of the dead in a disguised form." It seems to me not improbable that Kubary's theory gives us a synopsis of ordinary religious evolution, and that the Pelew Islanders afford a perfect example of typical religious history. Belief in the friendliness of ancestral spirits was prevalent also among the natives of the Ladrones.

Seligmann has shown that the primitive religion of the Veddas was essentially a cult of the dead. The Vedda, though he has little respect for a dead body, has a great desire to establish friendly relations with the departed spirits. His religious ceremonies have as their usual aim the possession of the living by the souls of the dead, and the state of frenzy or ecstacy which is thus induced cannot be said to differ in any way from the rapture of the saint or the disordered raving of the "medium." Bilindi Yaka, the being who is practically the god of the next world, and certainly the only godlike figure which the Veddas evolved, was, during his life on earth, a great hunter. Here again the course of religious development, moving logically from the cult of the dead to the establishment of a deistic belief, is plainly indicated; and the example is of much interest on account of the extremely primitive nature of the people affording it.

De Groot, in his admirable study of primitive Chinese

religion, says, " The ancestors no doubt were in East Asia the first gods, before mental development and culture had caused that part of the world to invent other *shen*." Again we find that the shades of ancestors were the protecting spirits of hearth and home ; that the house had its own altar, on which the dead were honoured ; that offerings were made on definite occasions and anniversaries—offerings which, in modern times, include paper images of slaves, wives, and concubines, which are ceremonially burnt : survivals of grimmer custom, in which the sacrifice was that of living persons.

The evidence which is derived from the study of existing primitive races is often supplemented by the evidence revealed through the study of the peoples of antiquity, and that is very true in the case of our present subject. The noble religion of dynastic Egypt was not merely based upon the cult of dead ancestors, it consisted largely in the perpetuation of that cult. It has been said that the great gods of Egypt were probably all of them evolved from deified ancestors ; and it is certain that the dominant and persistent aspect of Egyptian religion which is shown in the worship of Osiris, Lord of the Other World, is that which is immediately connected with the cult of the dead. The devotee of Osiris desired, above all things, to meet his own ancestors in the happy fields of the Tuat. In the chapels or tomb-chambers, those who were rich enough to do so presented costly and beautiful offerings to the shades of their forefathers ; and in those sanctuaries, made comely and familiar with bright pictures of the life of the deceased, the worshippers felt that they were in actual communion with their departed friends—a quiet, joyous, and deeply religious communion.

The soul of the Greek hero emerged from his tomb in the likeness of a snake, and Zeus himself, in his form of Meilichios, comes from the underworld as a serpent-god.

So the Olympian rose from the darkness and horror of the sepulchre. Afterwards, throned in the clouds or on the holy mountain, he looked with disapproval on the local divinities who, reaching the brink of the grave, aspired to the high places of godhead.

J. A. MacCulloch, examining the religion of the ancient Kelts, discovers everywhere traces of the ancestor-cult. " Fairy," he says, " corresponds in all respects to old ancestral ghost, and the one has succeeded to the place of the other, while the fairy is even said to be the ghost of a dead person." The ancestral god of the Kelts, their father-god, seems to have been Dispater, a chthonic divinity, ruling and residing in the world of shades. Like many other primitive folk, the Kelts drank the blood of their relatives, a purely religious form of communion—indeed, a true sacrament. When the Keltic warrior came back from raid or battle with human heads dangling from his belt, he offered those heads, not to any full-fledged god, but to the " strong shades " of his tribal heroes. As with the Greeks, the local heroes of the Kelts acquired, or aspired to, divine prestige. It was on the ancestral burial mounds that solemn rites were celebrated, and it was the hero who was ever thought of as the ghostly guardian of the clan. And precisely as the English troops of modern times have gone into action with the cry of " St. George ! " so the Keltic spearmen ran upon the foe with a shouting of strong names—the names of the ancestral heroes.

Had they lived in more ancient times, there is little doubt that Robin Hood, Cœur de Lion, and the Black Prince would have been elevated to the rank of first-rate tribal gods ; and, indeed, the same observation applies to Marlborough, Nelson, or any popular hero. As humanity advances, values undergo revision ; and it is this fact alone which has put a stop to the process of god-making and fixed the civilised world in dogged monotheism.

Whether or no the cult of gods is derived solely from the cult of the ancestral dead, it is manifest that the existence of gods is dependent on the existence of a belief in the immortality of the human soul—that the worship of the one cannot subsist without the belief in the other. The value of a god is, that he guarantees immortality, of which he is himself the proof and symbol. That all gods were once living men was the view of old Euhemerus in the third century before Christ; and that opinion was also maintained by Hesiod, Cicero, Alexander the Great, and Eusebius. It is a view that has always been severely criticised, but has never lacked advocates. " If man's soul really holds a fragment of god and is itself a divine being, its godhead cannot depend on the possession of great riches and armies and organised subordinates " (Gilbert Murray). But is not the Euhemeristic theory rather, that the soul of the mighty man possesses in an intensified degree those divine qualities which, in that degree alone, procure for the soul an immortality of power? At a given stage, but only at that stage, the soul has a survival value which entitles it to claim admittance to the company of the gods. We have already seen that there are primitive men who regard immortality, in any shape or form, as an aristocratic privilege. In primitive societies, it is certainly the memory of the powerful dead which gives birth to the gods who are worshipped by those societies : all the early gods are definitely anthropomorphic—they are, in fact, immortal men, with all the whims and jealousies and cruelties, all the desires and affections of ordinary people. Gods of the sun and the moon, of the woods or caverns or seas, are only located ancestral spirits. It is possible that such inventions have prepared the way for the revelation of a fuller truth. It is possible that the ultimate godhead exists as a concept apart altogether from the deified potentate. We are concerned here only with the worship of dead ancestors, and we are probably not mistaken in ascribing to that worship the germ of all religious thought and the creation of all the pristine gods.

MOURNING

The conduct of people at a funeral, as we all know, is not due entirely to the sensation of real grief. It is, indeed, largely due to mere propriety. With primitive folk it is due to something else, and something more powerful than grief or propriety—the desire to please the departed, and thus to keep him quiet and harmless. Unless we remember this, we might fall into the error of supposing that savages are the most affectionate of men, and that their frenzied behaviour at a death is caused by the urgings of uncontrollable sorrow. When a notable man died in the Society Islands, for example, the attitude was not " So the chief is dead ! Well, he was a good fellow, and we are sorry that we shall see no more of him," but rather, " So the chief is dead ! Let us howl and belabour ourselves, lest he be slighted, and visit us with his terrible wrath." As a result of this attitude, a ghastly pantomime has to be enacted, and this is inspired, not by affection or by grief, but by sheer terror, and its whole aim is to appease the ghost. In this pantomime the people of the tribe are compelled to take part ; those who are negligent or backward may be severely punished, or even killed. Such is the force of public opinion backed by public fear. Whether the near relatives of a dead man are sincerely affected by his loss, in any primitive community, is not at all certain ; the governing factor in the observance of primitive funeral rites is fear, and fear so powerful and pervading that there seems little room for any other sentiment.

Among the northern tribes of Australia, the widow had to observe rigorously the prescribed form and terms of mourning. She had to burn her hair, and cover herself with the ashes of the camp fire, and she had to maintain a strict silence. If she did not do these things, the ghost of her husband would tear her to pieces, or dispose of her in some other horrible way. But, as a matter of fact, the ghost had a valuable accessory in his younger brother, who, if he saw that the widow was not behaving properly, might thrash her, or actually put her to death. Widows had therefore every inducement to honour their social traditions. Among the Warramunga, the ban of silence applied to the wife, mother, sister, daughter, and mother-in-law of the deceased during the whole period covered by the funeral ceremonies, which might extend for two years or more ; so that " it was no uncommon thing to find that the greater number of women in any camp were prohibited from speaking " (Spencer and Gillen). Communication was effected by gestures. The silence might be voluntarily prolonged, and a case is recorded in which the widow had not spoken for upwards of twenty-five years. That such discipline should be found among utter savages may well excite our admiration, and perhaps our envy.

The most wonderful account of primitive mourning is that which is given by Spencer and Gillen in their book on the northern tribes of Central Australia. This account has peculiar value, for it comes from highly trained and competent witnesses, and as it is thoroughly typical of primitive observance and is written with admirable vigour, I cannot do better than transcribe a portion of it : A middle-aged man of the Warramunga tribe, who was a wizard, had transgressed in a matter of medical etiquette, and was dying. His illness, though doubtless caused by avenging spirits or by the working of hostile magic, had the appearance of being dysentery. As death approached, the men set up a dismal howling, and the camp of the dying man was speedily demolished. Some of the women lay on the sufferer's body, and others dug sharp yam-sticks into their heads till the blood streamed down all over them. Then a number of men rushed up and threw themselves on the body, from which the women rose, " until in a few minutes we could see nothing but a struggling mass of bodies all mixed up together." At this stage, a man of the Thapungarti class, advancing, slashed himself across the thigh muscles with a stone knife, so that he was unable to stand, and fell in the midst of the group. The self-wounded man was dragged out of the mêlée by his female relatives, who sucked the blood from his gashes, while he lay exhausted on the ground. " Gradually the struggling mass of dark bodies began to loosen, and then we could see that the man was not actually dead, though the terribly rough treatment to which he had been subjected had sealed his fate. . . . Later on in the evening, when the man actually died, the same scene was re-enacted, only this time the wailing was still louder, and men and women, apparently frantic with grief, were rushing about cutting themselves with knives and sharp-pointed sticks, the women battering one another's heads with fighting clubs, no one attempting to ward off either cuts or blows. Then . . . a small torchlight procession started off across the plain to a belt of timber a mile away, and there the body was left on a platform built of boughs in a low gum-tree." Next morning there was no trace of the dead man's camp, and the other camps were moved to a distance, so as to avoid contact with the ghost. Men were lying about with gashed thighs, like the wounded on a battlefield. The two widows had cut off all their hair, and, having smeared themselves with pipeclay, were sitting under a little shelter made of boughs. All the women relatives were wailing and cutting their scalps ; the other women, after a sham fight, were sitting in clusters, embracing each other and howling frantically. It was understood that any women who failed in the exact performance of these pious exercises would be heavily punished, or actually killed, by their brothers.

Burning or searing the flesh, as an alternative to laceration, was also practised by the Australians.

Self-laceration is a frequent practice among primitive mourners. It is an ancient practice, and is expressly condemned in the Book of Leviticus : " Ye shall not make any cuttings in your flesh for the dead."

Darwin, in his description of a Maori funeral, says, " The relatives of the family had torn the flesh of their arms, bodies, and faces, so that they were covered with clotted blood." The Tongans were not sparing in self-torture and mutilation at funerals : they pushed spear-heads into their sides and thighs ; they gashed themselves with shark's teeth, and the women cut off their fingers and slit their ears and noses ; teeth were knocked out with stones, and pates so heavily bethwacked with clubs that the sound of the blows was audible at a distance. The Society Islanders made special implements for these horrid purposes—implements with shark's teeth stuck into them. After the death of a Society Island notable, the chief mourner armed himself with one of these implements, and mauled and belaboured everyone who came within his reach, nor were his followers at all backward in the use of their clubs. At the demise of a Hawaiian king, people got worked up to such a pitch that they knocked their eyes out, twelve predestined retainers were slain, and the entire populace ran riot.

Instances of this frenzied, but really conventional, behaviour at funerals are to be found in all parts of the world. In some cases the conventional nature of the mourning is fully realised. A death in Dahomey was announced by piercing cries ; whereat the friends of the deceased ran to load their muskets, and proceeded to loose off a few volleys in his honour : at this, the wailing ceased, and gave place to jollity (Foà). Avowedly

hypocritical outbursts of grief are indulged in by the
Kai people of New Guinea, with the declared intention
of deceiving the ghost.

The Irish wake, in its later forms a nauseous and
drunken revel, had for its original purpose the placation
of the departed spirit. The observances of the wake were
long jealously maintained by the Irish peasant, because
he believed that any omission or carelessness would
expose him to the dead man's vengeance. In Wales,
the wake took a peculiar form, and is thus described by
Miss Trevelyan : " When the relatives and friends of
the deceased person had assembled, the coffin containing
the body was lifted on four men's shoulders. These
men then proceeded to tramp up and down the room
with slow and measured steps. Meanwhile the immediate relatives would hide their faces in their hands
and moan incessantly. . . . Hot spiced beer or hot
elderberry wine was handed round, and it was considered
unlucky if anybody refused a sip. The coffin was
frequently changed from one set of men to another, and
this proceeding was carried out all night. The purpose
of this strange custom was to scare away the evil spirits
. . . who were supposed to be lurking in dark corners
of the house to carry away the soul." The explanation is
not convincing : most probably it was the spirit of the
dead man himself that lurked in the dark corners, observing the behaviour of his friends.

The belief in immortality must have arisen, as we have
seen, from some common experience or experiences
which primitive man has accepted without hesitation
as proof of human survival. From this belief has
developed a cult of the dead, and of chthonic or underworld divinities. There are some who would affirm
that, in their upward progress, the dead and their
divinities have moved from power to power : perhaps,
from earth and underworld, they have risen to the

topmost heavens, have made themselves masters of the stars and rulers of the universe. Be that as it may, it is no easy matter to decide where ghost ends and god begins. Of this we are sure, that gods make their first appearance in the world of shades—they emerge from the tomb. And just as a common experience has inculcated the belief in the immortal, so a common sentiment has united men in their attitude towards the dead : the sentiment of fear. It is fear that seals the sepulchre, fear that binds or maims the body, fear that fills the grave with treasured property or with the victims of cruel sacrifice. It is through fear that man takes up the attitude of worship and seeks to propitiate the watchful and terrible dead. By vision born of fear men know the horrors of darkness, and by that vision they bear testimony to ghostly visits and ghostly actions. Through exceeding fear the dead are raised, first to the plane of the living and then above it ; and so it is along a pathway of fear that man approaches his hard-faced gods.

The original concept of immortality appears to have brought little if any comfort : men were less sustained by their hope of a future life than crushed by their fear of those who had already entered upon it. To-day we live under conditions which have deprived the ruling individual of real, unchallenged power, and which have robbed him of all his personal terrors. In our general attitude towards ghosts we are patronising, curious, sceptical, or merely silly. It is not easy for us to realise the intense conviction of the primitive mind. It is not easy for us to believe that the mental evolution of man leads him through a stage where the dead are the absolute lords and masters of the living. Yet we must realise and believe these things if we seek to understand the deep and distant origins of man's belief in the ghostly, his enslavement by gods and terrors of his own making, his tremendous faith in the immortal.

CHAPTER III

THE PREHISTORIC IMMORTAL

Prehistoric burials—Burials in the Stone Age—Burials in the Bronze Age—Burials in the Protohistoric Period.

PREHISTORIC BURIALS

IN matters archæological we are reminded continually of the limitations of our knowledge. When we travel back through the incalculably long prehistoric ages, we very soon reach the point at which relative certainty comes to an end, and doubt begins. We are forced to admit that we know very little about the early migrations of man, the differentiation of races, and the spread of culture. A general idea of sequence is all that we can claim. Archæology is essentially the study of problems (many of them to all appearance problems that can never be solved), and its findings undergo perpetual revision and readjustment. Some of our experts, indeed, are the first to confess their difficulties and uncertainties ; a confession which is sometimes made with a disconcerting degree of candour and with a noble disregard of criticism. Yet there is no study in which controversy is more prominent, or in the pursuit of which men spend more of their time in proving the absurdity of each other's opinions.

Now, of all the problems which confront the student of prehistoric man, the problem of chronology is one of the most perplexing. There is a reasonable certainty as regards the succession of cultures, but there is no certainty as regards the lapse of time during which those cultures have persisted.

The dating of the earliest prehistoric burials, therefore, can only be approximate. From the nature of the material which is found in a prehistoric grave, and from the nature of the overlying deposits, we obtain evidence which often enables us to assign that grave to its proper relative place in the story of cultural development. But we cannot go further. We cannot date it in terms of years. When we attempt to do so we may be five or ten thousand years wide of the mark. (In determining the age of the earliest human manufactures, allowance has to be made for a margin of error at least ten times as great.)

However, the evidence at our disposal justifies us in assuming that burial, in the full meaning of the word, was a practice well known to the Europeans of twenty thousand years ago. It was known to the Neanderthal people—a people who, in structure and poise, were more primitive and more emphatically simian than any existing race. This fact is one of the most extraordinary revelations of prehistory ; a fact so unexpected and of such deep significance that it was not readily admitted by anthropologists of the old school. It is largely due to the circumstance that they did bury their dead that we know what we do know of the Neanderthal race. Our knowledge of the greatly superior race which ousted the Neanderthal is also derived, to a very considerable extent, from the discovery of their graves ; and the same may be said in regard to all the succeeding prehistoric races. Every archæologist is by profession a plunderer of tombs.

In Egypt, a land full of great cemeteries and tombs and monuments, the prehistoric cult of the dead passes, with no essential change, into the fully elaborated religion of the dynastic periods. Egyptian beliefs and burial customs, concerning which we possess ample evidence, are therefore of surpassing interest. The richness and variety of the material which has been discovered and described by French and English workers in Egypt has led to the growth of a department of science —Egyptology—which has for its sole aim the collection, preservation, and description of Egyptian antiquities. We must reserve our survey of ancient Egyptian teachings and funeral rites (necessarily a most inadequate survey) for a separate chapter.

Prehistoric graves afford evidence of the anatomy, psychology, race, and social condition of the people whose bodies and belongings they contain. They are thus of particular interest from more than one point of view. We are concerned here mainly with their psychological interest. We shall deal rather with the construction, the contents and arrangement of the grave, and with the position of the bodies contained within it, than with the anatomical character of the human remains. Only in the case of Neanderthal man must the anatomical character be described in some detail, because, in his case, it has a very distinct and peculiar bearing on the psychological aspect. The description of archæological materal, of " grave furniture," and of the form of the tomb, is of great importance to us.

BURIAL IN THE STONE AGE

That mysterious creature, Neanderthal or Moustierian man, lived in Europe, or rather in such portions of it as were habitable, under what we should regard as extremely unpleasant conditions. He had to accustom himself, as the Moustierian centuries rolled on, to the increasing severities of a glacial epoch. Great sheets of ice spread gradually over the northern part of the continent and across the frozen seas. Immense glaciers pushed down from the Alpine ranges, the Pyrenees, and the Caucasus. In the sodden, cold, and desolate places where it was possible for them to subsist, there lived a number of hardy animals. The hairy mammoth with his long curving ivories, the cave bear, the woolly rhinoceros, the first Mid-European reindeer, the bison, scavenging wolves and foxes, the terrible cave lion and the cave hyena (survivors from the preceding warm period) were the contemporaries of Moustierian man. For some thousands of years, in fog and frost, in all the icy bleakness of a sub-Arctic region, amid the chill gloom of the tundra, this man made a successful stand against the horrible circumstances in which he had to maintain the struggle for existence. But, as conditions improved, he disappeared—and disappeared with some abruptness. Why? Did he withdraw from Europe? or did he fail in adaptability and so become extinct? or was he exterminated by a more advanced race? We cannot say. It is only necessary for our present purpose that we should know something about the appearance and habits of this ancient representative of humanity.

At the present day, there is no race, in any part of the world, which bears more than a partial or fortuitous resemblance to the Neanderthal. A sham Neanderthal feature may crop up here and there, but in no case have we that assemblage of peculiar features which would justify us in recognising the true Neanderthal type. When we try to visualise that type, our reconstruction is based on the study of skeletal remains, of which, fortunately, we now possess many fine specimens. But such a reconstruction, if too detailed, has only a relative value ; for it must be remembered, that more than one sort of countenance and more than one sort of carcase may be modelled over the same skull and skeleton. The general outline, however, is determined by the bony framework, and the general outline of Neanderthal man may be described with some accuracy.

In the bones of his skull, his limbs, his vertebral column—indeed, in practically every part of his skeleton —we find peculiarities which are not present in any other known variety of the human stock. All those peculiarities are of a kind which is reminiscent of the ape. He is distinctly human ; yet, in making comparisons, we push him instinctively into the neighbourhood of the anthropoid apes, just as we push his Aurignacian successor into the neighbourhood of modern man. In figure, he was short and massive. His head, which was large, not only in relation to his body but in relation to the heads of modern people, was supported by an enormously thick neck. The upper part of his body was bent forward, and the head, viewed from in front, had a tendency to sink between the great width of the shoulders. His legs were very short, and permanently bent at the knee ; he walked with a shuffling gait, and was structurally incapable of standing erect. The skull is long from back to front ; it is characterised by the flatness of the cranial vault, by the extension of the hinder part, and by the great ridges of bone which overhang the eye-sockets. In general form, it may be compared, so far as the cranial part is concerned, to a cast of a modern skull as it would appear if squashed by vertical pressure. The eye-sockets are large and deep, the nasal cavities are wide, and the sub-nasal region is broad and " inflated "—that is, pushed out like the muzzle of an ape. The cheek-bones are flat and retreating. In the lower jaw, the primitive character is strongly emphasised : the ascending ramus is extraordinarily wide and massive, while the profile line, from the teeth to the point of the jaw, recedes inwards like the bow of a rowing-boat. Yet the teeth and palate are highly specialised, and, according to Sir Arthur Keith, are less ape-like than those of modern man.

So here is a creature more brutish, more primitive than the lowest of existing peoples ; a human creature, but a human creature of a type that was apparently doomed to perish because it was unable to adapt itself to the conditions which have produced the modern type. Moustierian man lived in caves for preference, surrounded by masses of putrid refuse. He had learnt how to make use of fire ; and he was able to produce flint implements which show that he was a dexterous and experienced knapper. But he could go no further. For some ten thousand years, it would seem, he had made no intellectual advance. The final decay and obliteration of the Moustierian race must have occurred not later than twenty thousand years ago.

This bent, clumsy, shuffling figure, living under such dismal and squalid conditions, struggling for so long only to be extinguished in the end, has, if you will, an almost pathetic interest. He was a failure. He was too primitive to last. And now observe what is, perhaps, the most amazing thing about him—he buried his dead, not only with care, but with appropriate gifts or property. He must have believed that he was immortal.

A little cave near the village of La Chapelle-aux-Saints in the Corrèze was explored in 1908 by three priests—the Abbés A. and J. Bouyssonie and L. Bardon. They had already found a great number of Moustierian flint implements when, on August the third, they discovered a buried skeleton. That skeleton is now one of the most famous in the world. It has been wonderfully described in a monograph by M. Boule, the most eminent of all living experts on human palæontology. It has a classic reputation for all students of prehistoric man as one of the most carefully exhumed, most complete, and most characteristic of Neanderthal skeletons. But, for us, its great significance is, that it afforded one of the most valuable and unmistakable proofs of the practice of burial in the Moustierian age.

The skeleton of La Chapelle is that of an adult male, some forty-five years of age ; and, like all his race, of short stature. The body had been placed in a small, shallow pit, sunk beneath the ancient floor of the cave : it lay on its back, with both legs bent to the right, the right arm flexed and the left extended. The head had been carefully protected by an arrangement of stones, and near it were the bones of the leg of an ox. Close to the body were many fine flint implements—points and scrapers—of the Moustierian type, together with fragments of quartz, scraps of ochre, and pieces of bone. Just inside the cave (which was so small that it could never have been a commodious habitation) there were traces of a hearth. At the entrance there was a small trench containing bison bones and a flint point, covered by blocks of limestone. All this is suggestive of ritual, and invites the imagination; an invitation which, though alluring, is not of the kind that we can accept with prudence.

There is no doubt whatever that we are here dealing with an extremely ancient burial. In the details of this burial we discover something more than the mere desire to protect the body ; we discover objects which, in their association with the body, imply a clear belief in the spiritual existence of the deceased.

Neither is the burial at La Chapelle a solitary example. Just a week after the extraction of the La Chapelle skeleton, a band of marauding German scientists, summoned by their jackal, Hauser, removed a skeleton from Le Moustier itself. The skeleton was that of a lad, probably about seventeen years of age, showing all the characteristic Neanderthal features. He had been carefully buried. His body had been laid on the right side, the left arm stretched out and the right bent back under the head. Beneath the head were some stones, and it appeared as if the nose had been protected by flint flakes. Within reach of the left hand was a remarkably fine example of a flint weapon. A number of flint implements were in contact with the body, and near it were the charred and split bones of an ox. It will be noted that there are certain points of resemblance between this burial and that of La Chapelle.

Further points of resemblance occur in the Moustierian burials at La Ferrassie (Dordogne), the first of which was discovered by Peyrony in 1909. Again we find a body with the head protected by a stone ; again the body is on its back, legs bent to the right, left arm straight and right arm flexed. And also, as at La Chapelle, a little trench seems to have been dug to contain the bone of an animal—this time, of a large cow. It has been suggested, however, that the bodies at La Ferrassie were not inhumed ; that they were merely covered with earth as they lay on the cave floor. A similar treatment has been suggested with reference to the celebrated Spy skeletons (1886).

We have thus evidence of the care of the dead, if not of an actual cult, in remote palæolithic times ; and I think we shall not be mistaken in assuming that this care of the dead must have been in existence at least two score thousand years ago. The great importance of these palæolithic burials, both from the philosophic and psychological points of view, cannot very well be exaggerated. And when we consider that a form of man, more highly evolved in every respect than the Neanderthal, was living in some other part of the world while the Neanderthal people were living in Europe, we shall realise that the dawn of the belief in immortality must have occurred in times so far distant as to lie beyond any effort of calculation.

That a more highly evolved form of man was produced elsewhere, before the Neanderthal occupation of Europe, is shown by the relatively sudden advance of this form into the European area. This new and improved man is known as the Cro-Magnon. From the physical standpoint, he has never been surpassed. He was tall and shapely, a trifle long in leg and forearm, with a high forehead and a wide massive countenance. He marched with an erect carriage. He had reached that level of primitive culture which produces art, and gives a great deal of thought to personal adornment. He is the direct ancestor of the modern European.

The fact that burial occurred in palæolithic times was first proved by the discovery of Cro-Magnon burials in the Red Caves of Mentone. Here, in 1872, Rivière, excavating the Grotte du Cavillon, discovered the famous *Homme du Menton;* and in 1874 and 1875 further discoveries were made. Prince Albert of Monaco interested himself in the Mentone caves in 1883, and by 1895 he had organised, with noble enthusiasm, a little band of learned and capable men. Between 1895 and 1902, Prince Albert and his associates made a series of discoveries which are among the most important in the records of prehistoric archæology.

The skeleton found by Rivière lay beneath a deposit of stalagmite. It was that of a tall man, placed on the left side, with legs slightly bent, and both hands raised to the level of the throat. The whole skeleton and the ornaments found with it were stained with powdered red ochre. In front of the face there was a sort of groove, about seven inches long, containing a supply of red ochre. On the head there was a fillet of threaded shells (nassa neritea). A bodkin of stag bone lay across the brow, and close to the temples were twenty-two pierced reindeer teeth. Two flint flakes were tilted against the back of the head.

The bodies whose remains were found in the later excavations had been more richly bedecked. Among other burials in the Barma Grande cave were those of a tall man, an immature woman, and a boy. The pit in which these remains had been placed was full of a red ochreous powder : the bodies were extended, or only gently flexed. On the man's head had been placed a coronet of deer canines, fish vertebræ, and small pierced shells ; on his neck was a gorget of the same materials. By his side was a flint knife. The woman's head was propped on the thigh-bone of an ox : her ornaments were similar to those of the man, but less pretentious, and in her hand she held a flint blade over ten inches long. The boy wore an elaborate crown of fish vertebræ and shells, divided in groups by deer's teeth. In the same cave there was found the skeleton of a man on its back, the legs crossed at the shins, both arms bent, and the left hand on the breast. This man had been decorated with a collar of shells ; he had a large piece of gypsum near his left hand; and the usual deer canines, together with small ivory pendants, were found in various places. It is stated that a burnt burial, in too disintegrated a condition to be properly examined, was found in this cave.

Of Cro-Magnon burials of the later period (Magdalenian) we may mention that found at Brünn in Moravia. The skeleton was that of a man fifty-five to sixty years of age, and of short stature. The arms were raised ; the left hand under the head, and the right hand under the left side of the lower jaw. The feet were drawn up towards the pelvis, and the knees touched the teeth— the body was therefore strongly contracted. In association with the body there was a large mammoth tusk, and there were also six hundred bits of shell (dentalium badense) cut and shaped, fourteen discs made of red sandstone and quartzite, of rhinoceros bone and ivory, some of them pierced and ornamented with strokes and notches, an instrument of stag horn, and a much battered ivory statuette. This statuette, and the bones of the skeleton also, had been stained with some ochreous substance. Another Moravian grave, discovered by Maschka in 1894, contained no fewer than fourteen complete skeletons and the remains of six more, protected by stones.

A singular burial of Magdalenian age was found in the Grotte des Hoteaux, near Rousillon (Ain), by Tournier and Guillon in 1894. In the grave had been placed, not a body, but only the bones of one ; and those bones were not laid out in their correct anatomical position. The skull was wrongly placed in relation to the spine, and the bones of the spine were wrongly placed in relation to each other ; while the right thigh-bone was in the left hip socket, and vice versa. The remains were those of a lad of sixteen to eighteen years old. With him there were perforated pecten shells and teeth, bone pins and needles, typical Magdalenian flints, and an implement with an engraving of a stag. The bones lay in a bed of red ochre. This seems to be an instance of a practice which is not unusual among living savages—the practice of removing all the soft parts of the body and of placing the bones alone within the grave.

Other interesting Magdalenian burials have been discovered at Sordes (Landes), at Obercassel, near Bonn, and at Raymonden, near Chancelade ; but we cannot examine these in detail. It suffices for our purpose to show that the Europeans of upper palæolithic times, like the Moustierians who lived before them, buried their dead. It is significant, that the Cro-Magnon people adorned the dead body with objects which must have had the highest value for the living. This may be regarded as proof that their attitude towards the departed was based on a fully evolved conviction and on a clear and detailed belief in spiritual existence.

The culture of the New Stone Age—the neolithic period—seems to correspond everywhere with an intensified cult of the dead. Whether he is regarded with fear or affection, or with reverence compounded of both, the lordship of the ghost appears to be well-nigh absolute. To this age belong the massive stone burial chambers, the dolmens ; structures which must have demanded prodigious labour on the part of the builders, and which testify to communal discipline of a high order, or to the compelling influence of cult. Dolmens are the oldest of all surviving human constructions, and it is notable that they were raised for the protection and commemoration of the dead ; one might say, for the residence

of the dead. The men who built the dolmens had
no such residences. They lived in pit-dwellings, in
caves, in huts of mud and wattle, or in rude shelters
of a like sort.

Dolmens, and the forms of passage or chamber derived
from or associated with them, are constructions of the
simplest kind. An ideal dolmen consists of a quadrangular enclosure, made by setting up four slabs of
stone and placing a covering stone across the tops of
them. This chamber, having the earth for its floor,
a single stone for each wall and a single stone for the roof,
contains the bodies of the illustrious dead, with such
provision and accompaniments as are proper to their
rank. After it has received its contents, stones and earth
are heaped over it, but not necessarily to a great height.
It is by no means certain that every dolmen was originally covered in this manner.

From the simple dolmen is derived the " covered
alley," with or without side-chambers—or the dolmen
itself may have a *dromos* or approaching corridor.
The " kist," of dolmenic origin, is a smaller form of the
enclosed chamber. In the great mounds or " barrows "
of neolithic date, which are not infrequently met with
in parts of the British Isles and in Scandinavia, there
are usually several kists or galleries, not necessarily
connected with each other, and almost invariably one
large chamber in the centre of the broad end of the
barrow. Occasionally one of the side stones of a dolmenic burial chamber is pierced by a round counter-
sunk hole, or a hole is formed by juxtaposing two slabs
with a semi-circular slice cut out of each. It cannot
be doubted that these holes were intended for the convenience of the imprisoned spirit. Such holes are not
often found in European dolmens, though there are
several examples in the neighbourhood of Paris, but they
occur with great frequency among the Indian dolmens
of the Deccan country.

Dolmens are found in Japan and Korea, India, Syria, the Caucasian region, along the shores of the Black Sea, in parts of Russia, in Asia Minor, Thrace, Northern Africa, Italy, Malta, Spain, France, the British Isles, Belgium and Holland, Northern Germany, and the southern parts of Scandinavia. They are not found in Crete, Greece, Sicily, Sardinia, and Central Europe. France alone possesses over 4,400 dolmens.

These ancient monuments (the true dolmens) contained usually one or two bodies. The " grave furniture " included such things as pendants of shell and ivory, necklaces made of stone or bone beads, or of clay balls and fish vertebræ strung together ; bone implements, stone axes (sometimes showing traces of fire), flint blades and arrow-heads, scrapers and flakes, and various types of pottery vessels. But by far the greater number of the discovered neolithic burials are those which were placed within the kists and passage chambers of the barrows or the cemeteries. Of these, some contain the complete skeleton of an individual, or the complete skeletons of more than one individual, with the bones in their normal relation to each other ; thus affording proof of the burial of entire bodies. Others are full of the scattered and broken remains of several people, often mixed with the bones of animals, in a space far too small to have held their complete bodies ; moreover, it is often found, in such cases, that no complete skeleton is present. Such a burial, if undisturbed, gives us proof that only parts of bodies or parts of skeletons were placed within the tomb. However, there are cases in which entire skeletons have been found in contact with the dispersed or incomplete remains of others ; though we cannot be sure that the entire skeletons, in such instances, are not intruders. Where the jumbled-up bones of a number of people clearly represent the original interment, in a grave which could never have contained the whole carcases of those people, we can only explain matters by advancing one or the other of the following theories : (*a*) the tomb is an ossuary, a place intended to receive the bones of those whose bodies had undergone the stages of a progressive ritual, or who had died in some distant place ; or (*b*) portions of the dead bodies were retained for some purpose of cult, which may have implied that they were eaten or preserved, while other portions were stuffed into the tomb. I have myself excavated an undisturbed kist burial, where, in a chamber measuring about three by four feet and less than four feet deep, the bones represented the remains of four fully-grown persons, two young children, an ox, a horse, a dog, and a pig.

Red colouring matter is sometimes found in neolithic graves, usually in the form of ochre, iron oxides (such as limonite), or cinnabar. Pots of red cosmetic have been found in the tombs at Terranova in Italy ; and in the Ligurian region, the entire grave was often filled with red ochre. A skeleton found in one of the kists at Chamblandes (near Lausanne) held a morsel of red ochre in its right hand.

Very frequently, chips and flakes of flint, and sherds of pottery, are found scattered throughout the funerary deposit in neolithic tombs. It has been assumed that these fragments are the result of a ceremonial flaking of flint and smashing of pots at the time of the burial ; but this conjecture, though plausible, does not necessarily offer the true explanation. The flints may have been regarded as valuable or useful property, and the pottery may have been broken through the accidental disturbance of the grave. It must be admitted, however, that it is seldom possible to reconstruct a complete pot from the sherds.

The neolithic cemetery at Chamblandes is of much interest. In nearly every example the kists (small ones, and formed of thin slabs) held the remains of two skeletons—that of a man, whose body had been placed in the tomb before the second one was added, and that of a woman. We can only account for the regularity of this by supposing that the women were killed or buried alive, in order that they might accompany their owners. In two cases, the body of a small child had been added. All the bodies in the Chamblandes cemetery were in the crouched position, and some of them wore pectorals of boar's tusks and of shells. Another cemetery was found in the island of Thinic (Morbihan in Brittany), containing twenty-seven small burial chambers, with skeletons in about half of them. The burials consisted usually of one or two bodies, in a few cases as many as four, superposed, and for the most part in the contracted position. The general orientation of these bodies was with the head to the south or south-east.

Perhaps the most remarkable of all neolithic burials in Europe are those in the artificial grottos of the Marne area. Although these grottos were known in 1816, they were not methodically explored until 1872, when they were taken in hand by the enthusiastic Baron de Baye. These extraordinary tombs are cut into chalky banks, a kind of trench leading to the mortuary chamber. Occasionally there are steps, which seem to have been much used. On the walls of several of the grottos the so-called " goddess of the tombs " makes her miserable appearance. This most inept caricature of the female form, rudely sculptured in relief, represents, in the opinion of Déchelette, an immigrant deity who found her way to France from Asia Minor. The tombs were either single or double ; that is, with or without an antechamber. The burials were almost invariably those of complete bodies. In tombs of the single-chamber type, the bodies had been laid out in two ranks, with a clear passage between them ; sometimes several layers of bodies were superposed in this order, the layers being separated, in certain cases, by the inter-position of stone slabs or sand. Piled bodies which were

not thus separated were invariably those of males.
Most commonly, the chambers contained the skeletons
of folk of both sexes and of all ages, covered with cinders
and fine earth. In the deeper of the single-chambered
grottos, and in those with two chambers, there were
rarely more than eight burials. Certain chambers,
large enough for some hundreds of bodies, contained
only those of two or three individuals. Among the two
thousand burials which were discovered in these grottos
there was only one solitary instance of the crouched
position : nearly all the bodies had been laid out
straight, with the arms by the sides. The burials had
been furnished with axes of flint and jadeite, some of
which were still in their horn hafts, with flint arrow-
heads and scrapers, worked bones, and occasional
ornaments, including a number of perforated *rondelles*
made from the bones of the human skull. There was
an abundance of pottery. Several skulls were found
which had been filled, after the decay or removal of the
brain, with miscellaneous rubbish, and, among it, small
manufactured objects and the bones of very young
children. This strange proceeding is not to be explained
by reference to similar practice elsewhere—at least, I do
not know of a similar practice—and we must therefore
regard it as unaccountable.

The neolithic people in Europe continued the extremely
ancient custom of burial in caves, or beneath the shelter
of overhanging rocks. It would appear that a cave was
sometimes occupied by the dead and the living at the
same time, and sometimes by dead and living alternately,
or again, exclusively by the dead. Many of these
funerary caves were closed with blocks of stone or with
a single great slab.

There is evidence which tends to prove that the men
of the New Stone Age were not unacquainted with the
gruesome procedure known to French archæologists as
décharnement présepulchral—the removal of the flesh

from the bones before the burial of the latter. We have seen that the later palæolithic folk appear to have done the same thing, at any rate occasionally ; and we know that the practice occurs very frequently among the uncivilised races of modern times. It will be remembered, that the motive commonly alleged in such cases is, the desire to release the spirit from its fleshly encumbrance and to free it, once for all, from corporal disability and restraint.

Cremation, the introduction of which was, at one time, ascribed loosely to the first users of metal, occurred sporadically and locally among the neolithic tribes.

BURIAL IN THE BRONZE AGE

Our knowledge of prehistoric man in general is but a fragmentary knowledge : our information with regard to prehistoric man outside Europe is woefully inadequate. That inadequacy is nowhere more evident than in matters pertaining to the introduction and first use of metals. In the early days of archæology, men would settle the question by pointing with a somewhat vague gesture towards the east. A gesture, however, is not an explanation. We are still in ignorance as to the original discovery or discoveries of metals, but we know that the metal cultures only replaced the stone cultures by slow and gradual stages. There was no swift substitution. The first metal implements were flat axes, made by pouring molten copper into a stone mould. They were reproductions of the more ancient axe-heads in stone, known as " celts," and it should be noted that stone implements were in use concurrently with metal implements, in all parts of the world, for many centuries after the introduction of copper.

The term " Bronze Age " is employed, in the popular sense, to denote that stage of human culture which is marked by the increasing use and currency of metals. Copper precedes bronze as a worked metal, and it is

probable that gold precedes copper. But the Bronze
Age, in its more significant aspect, is the period of great
racial movements. Those movements gradually brought
the Aryan-speaking peoples into prominence in Central
and Western Europe, and gradually spread among those
peoples the influences of that mysterious civilisation
which was developing in the more tranquil countries
bordering on the Eastern Mediterranean and among the
islands of the Ægean Sea.

As a result of growing complexity in the social structure and a consequent extension of social energies,
thoughts and customs began to change more rapidly
than they had done in the Age of Stone. And so we
find that the form of burial, in Europe, changes, howbeit
gradually, along with the other customs. The cult of
the dead, though not of less importance, appears to
become a more specialised, a more sophisticated part
of the social scheme. The simple deified ancestor has
spread himself out, as it were, and theological invention
is already at work. Gods of the earth, the sun, the corn-
field, the sea and the rivers, gods of generation, elemental
gods—all of them, perhaps, merely ancestors in their
most transcendent form—help to destroy the ancient
sovereignty of the ghost. Symbolism, and the growth
of esoteric ideals, tend to widen, and at the same time
to specialise, the spiritual outlook. The bases are
already laid, for religion on the one hand and for
scepticism on the other. Under these conditions, the
care of the dead, who, as such, are feared no less than
formerly, becomes a matter rather of policy and of
obligation than of compelling impulse. Forms of burial
vary, and, although they become more elaborate and
more richly furnished, they tend to assume a more
conventional character and to lose the massive dignity
of the older tombs.

Throughout the Bronze Age, burial customs in the
Levant show a bewildering diversity. Cremation was

in vogue at different places and at different times : it was never the exclusive rite. In Cyprus, one of the most important centres of the early metal industry, no cremated remains have been found in a tomb of Bronze Age date. In the island of Amorgus, the people used to push their dead into great jars ; a practice which occurred also in parts of Spain and among the Balearic Islands. The Thracians kept the body lying in state for three days, after which it was either burnt or buried, and a mound was raised over its remains. But in whichever way the body was disposed of, it became the object of " tendance," if not of cult ; for a hole was left in the mound, and through this hole supplies of food and drink were passed into the tomb. (A most singular example of this kind of tendance was revealed by certain Roman tombs at Carthage, where arrangements had been made for pouring liquid into the urns which contained the ashes of the dead.)

Inhumation was certainly the Athenian practice down to 600 B.C. At Palaikastro, in Crete, human remains were found in peculiar earthenware receptacles, of a shape and size resembling those of a modern bath ; while others were in square-cornered coffins, also of earthenware, with panelled sides, and resting on four short feet. These are known as *larnax* burials. Sometimes the larnax contained the bones of three people, although it could not have contained their entire bodies : in other cases, there were only skulls within it. The Cretan cemeteries of later date have chambers cut in the rock, shaft-graves, and pit-graves—the latter reminding one of the Egyptian *mastaba*.

It was at Mycenæ that the ancient civilisation of the Ægean countries reached one of its highest levels of barbarian magnificence. The royal tombs of Mycenæ were excavated by Schliemann ; a man whose genius for discovery and whose noble enthusiasm atoned, in some measure, for his deplorable lack of science. His interest in archæology was primarily a romantic interest. He was not so much concerned with the full significance of what he found as he was with the sheer joy of finding it. Consequently, his account of the Mycenæan tombs is a very incomplete account. We learn, from him, a great deal about the furniture of the tombs, but very little about the position and state of the skeletons which they contained, and practically nothing about the human type represented by those skeletons.

No other prehistoric burial place equals, in wealth and interest, the royal necropolis of Mycenæ. From Schliemann's account I take, in abridged form, the following characteristic details :

In the " fourth " tomb, which may be selected as the richest and most typical, the bodies of five men had been cremated on a prepared floor of pebbles. The bones were " literally smothered in jewels, all of which . . . show unequivocal marks of the funeral fires." After cremation, the bodies had been covered by a layer of white clay, and over this was a second layer of pebbles. The chamber was 26½ feet below the surface ; it was 24 feet long and 18½ feet broad, cut into the solid rock to a depth varying from 6 to 10 feet. The extraordinary richness, beauty, and variety of the " grave furniture " can only be conveyed by a fairly complete description of the contents of the tomb :

The whole sepulchre appears to have been strewn with small leaves of gold, scattered thickly before the burning of the bodies. Masks of gold, realistically modelled, had been pressed down over the faces of three of the skeletons ; while two of the bodies had breastplates, one had a fine golden tiara, and on the leg-bone of another was a strip of gold which had formed the fastening of a greave. At the left side of one of the bodies was a pile of 400 amber beads, pierced ; and in contact with the bones of all five bodies, or near them, were 110 golden flowers. There were five big copper vessels, in one of which were 100 wooden discs covered with thin plates of gold. There was a cow's head in silver, with long golden horns. Scattered through a great heap of bronze swords and lances were round plates of gold with intaglio work. The majority of the objects found near the bodies were either made of or plated with gold—signet rings, goblets, a bracelet and a shoulder belt, four large and two small diadems, a fillet and a waist-belt, ribbon, pins and rings, charms and ornaments, 256 buttons of various sizes, 232 plates with *répoussé* work, three models of temples or altars, a great variety of miscellaneous objects, an open-work cylinder and part of a dragon, both inlaid with flakes of rock-crystal—all of gold. There were also three hand-made terra-cotta vases, two objects of unknown use said to be made of Egyptian faïence, an alabaster model of a scarf tied in a noose, a silver wine flagon of beautiful design, fourteen objects of rock-crystal, and an alabaster vase with three handles. Moreover, there were copper tools, bone discs, wooden lozenges, eighteen silver vessels plated with copper, arrow-heads of obsidian, boar's teeth, the fragments of innumerable pots, and twenty-seven kettles, cans and basins of copper, together with a copper tripod. And, finally, many oyster shells, and " entire oysters which had never been opened."

No such profusion of barbaric finery is found in the Bronze Age graves of Central and Western Europe. Golden torques and gorgets, and other objects of gold occur but rarely ; though it has been shrewdly noted by Déchelette that, whereas the treasures of the Mycenæan tombs consisted largely of gold beaten into thin plates, the objects fashioned of that metal in the west are for the most part of a heavy and massive order.

With the introduction and diffusion of metals, and the accompanying racial and social changes, the rites of burial and the form of the tomb in Western Europe underwent considerable modification. The dolmen was replaced by a small kist, the walls of which were often built with blocks of stone, instead of being formed by single slabs. Long barrows were superseded by barrows of more or less circular plan, having the principal burial chamber in the centre, and other burials placed at random within the periphery. Vaulted or corbelled chambers make their appearance, recalling the cupola tombs of the Ægean countries. Cremation was widely, but never exclusively, practised, and the ashes were often placed in pottery vessels which are known as cinerary urns. These urns, singly or in groups, are generally found in small kists, or merely protected by two or three flat stones. Planks of wood were used in the construction of graves, and coffins made out of tree-trunks are not uncommon in certain areas. The furniture of the tomb was simple, and did not often comprise a great variety of objects. We do not find that the custom of colouring the bones of the dead is much in evidence ; neither are there many instances of the collection of bones in ossuaries. A certain number of coloured skeletons of Bronze Age date have been discovered, and the brothers Siret describe a skull from Aryar which had a band of vermilion painted across the brows like a diadem.

British archæologists are much indebted to Canon Greenwell, whose excavations of barrows on the Yorkshire Wolds and elsewhere were conducted, not only with zeal, but with admirable care and method. He recognised the importance of accurate record, and of noting carefully the exact position and arrangement of the human remains. From our point of view, his book (published in 1877) is remarkably interesting and instructive. In the whole vast range of archæological literature there is nothing of greater value for the student of barrow burials, and very little of equal value.

As regards British barrows, the following particulars are derived mainly from Greenwell's work.

The typical Bronze Age barrow resembles, in elevation, the form of an inverted bowl. It is sometimes surrounded by a circular ditch and a bank. Round barrows are almost invariably made of the materials found on the site—blocks of stone, sandy soil and flints, chalk, rubble, and so forth. Occasionally the burial is placed within a pit or depression sunk in the undisturbed soil below the centre of the mound.

In his general comments on the mound burials of the Yorkshire Wolds, Canon Greenwell observes that a great number of animal bones were usually found associated with the human remains. He records the fact that the secondary or additional burials were nearly always discovered on the south and east sides of the barrow ; rarely on the north and west sides. In the majority of cases, the body was not enclosed or protected in any way. Sometimes the grave had been floored with wood, and occasionally there were traces of wooden sides or roof. Here, as elsewhere, there was evidence to show that the body, when cremated, had seldom been burnt on the site of the tomb : the ashes had been carried to the grave from some other place, whether in the funerary urn, or in a wrapping of skins, or by some other means. But in certain cases, the calcined remains had been actually buried on or near the place of the burning. There were instances where " the bones were not collected after the burning, but were left in the position they had occupied before the fire was applied." The condition of some of the unburnt burials would seem to justify the supposition that the flesh had been removed from the bones before their entombment. " It is probable, however, that in the disturbed, disjointed, and incomplete skeletons we have the result of more than one practice." Of the burials examined by Greenwell, only twenty per cent were cremated. It is very noteworthy that, of three hundred and one burials of unburnt bodies, all save four had been placed in the contracted position ; and he was impressed by the fact, to which I have already drawn attention, that the crouched posture could not be explained on the ground that it was a device for economising space or labour. The arms and hands were arranged without any regard either for uniformity or for symmetrical adjustment : sometimes both hands were raised to the face, or placed on the top of the head ; sometimes they were pressed against the lower part of the stomach or bent under the hips ; or one hand might be on the head and the other on the breast or thigh. The bodies were laid indifferently on the right or left side, with a slight preference for the left.

The following particulars serve well to illustrate the funeral practices of the Bronze Age people of the Wolds, and elsewhere :

A singularly interesting barrow was excavated in Ganton parish (East Riding). This barrow, which was 60 feet in diameter, contained the bones of five very young children, the eldest of whom was about six years of age. It contained also the imperfectly burnt bones of an adult, probably a woman, the unburnt remains of two other women and of a young man about twenty-five years old. At the centre was an oval grave, within which lay the skeleton of a youth, together with the split bones of six oxen. But the most striking discovery was that of a double inhumation, fifteen feet east-north-east of the centre of the tumulus. Here had been deposited two bodies facing each other ; that of a man, some twenty years old, and that of a girl of about seventeen. The man's body had been laid partly over the other, and it seemed that the girl had been so placed that she clasped his head between her hands. The left hand of the youth was under his hip, and his right hand rested on the hip of his companion. Between the bodies were two food-vessels, each provided with a cover.

Such a burial affords a theme for sentiment or imagination ; and we cannot but see in it the expression of the hope that those who had been happy lovers on earth would be happy lovers in the world of the dead. Be that as it may, it is proof of the intention that a man should not be deprived by death of the companionship of one who had been dear to him in life ; and whether the woman had followed her master willingly, or whether she had been killed, or whether both had fallen victims to disease or to some act of savage retribution, that intention is clear.

Burials of children are frequently discovered in these barrows. They are often accompanied by their mother, who embraces or touches them, and in one case (at Willerby) Greenwell found that the original burial of a man with two children had been followed by the deposit in the same grave of a woman with two more children. It should be noted, that the bodies of infants, like those of adults, were almost invariably placed in the crouched position. Even the little flitting ghost of a child, we may infer, was thought of as a thing unwelcome and fearful.

At Weaverthorpe, a mound 80 feet in diameter was found to contain animal bones in a good state of preservation, sixteen flint scrapers, a saw and many flakes of flint, fragments of pottery, and the two halves of a red deer's antler, but no trace whatever of a human burial. In some of the barrows were mysterious holes or pits, near the burials, filled with burnt earth and charcoal, with unburnt human bones, and with bits of pottery. Relics, perhaps, of sacrifice. Sometimes there was evidence which proved that skeletons had been displaced and re-deposited, with clumsy attempts to get the bones into their proper order. Dispersed remains, in such instances, must not be confused with those which are found within the true ossuary. At Goodmanham a tumulus of 56 feet diameter held but one solitary burial—the burnt bones of a child of eight, who had been cremated on the spot.

Whether sacrifices were made at the funerals of children is a question which we cannot readily answer ; but sacrifice on such an occasion, if the child was the offspring of some important man, would be perfectly consistent with the views and practices of a savage people, and it may, perhaps, be indicated by the following evidence : In the centre of a barrow at Helperthorpe, which held several interments, burnt and unburnt, three skulls, touching each other, and laid out on a triangular plan, were placed near the burial of a two-and-a-half-years-old baby. A large barrow at Rudstone—100 feet in diameter and 9 feet high—contained the bodies of no fewer than ten children, though two of these may have been comparatively recent additions, and of some half-dozen adults, excluding five men who were regarded by Greenwell as intruders : but the primary interment was that of a child scarcely one year old. Again, in the parish of Ford in Northumberland, a small barrow enclosed the remains of a child about two years of age in a stone kist, and round the kist were placed six burnt bodies in as many urns.

An exceptional posture of a skeleton was noted at Rudstone. Among a number of burials in a large mound were the remains of a woman, lying on her left side ; but the knees " were turned in the opposite direction, as if the body, having been laid upon the left side, had been held firm in that position, whilst the legs were violently wrenched round until they were brought into the position they would have occupied had the body been laid upon the right side." Is it possible that this was a premature burial ?

The clothes worn by Bronze Age people have been actually found in their tree-trunk coffins. Of such discoveries, the most notable was made in the tumulus of Borun Eshoi in Jutland, where the dress of a woman was preserved : a knitted woollen cap, a jacket with short sleeves, and a long robe, secured by a belt with

tassels. Canon Greenwell found an oaken coffin in a
barrow at Rylston ; a coffin made from a log split in
two and hollowed out. Hardly a vestige of the body
was left, but there were traces of a woollen fabric in
which it had been wrapped from head to foot.

BURIAL IN THE PROTOHISTORIC PERIOD

As the extent and variety of individual property
increases, the objects placed with the dead become more
numerous and more highly finished. During the Iron
Age, in Europe, although the stone-lined tomb within
or beneath the tumulus is still the ordinary form of the
sepulchre, the furniture is richer and more elaborate
than it was during the preceding period.

The Gaulish warrior lies between the wheels of his
chariot. He is armed with sword and spear, and defended
by a buckler. On his brow he wears a circlet of flashing
gold, while beads of amber and ivory add splendour
to his attire. A flagon of Greek wine makes him brave
and cheerful, so that he is not dismayed by the tremendous rulers of the underworld. Solid sustenance he has
also—poultry and game, or joints of beef and pork. At his
feet are the trappings of his horses. Kingly in life, he is
kingly in the tomb, and with good cheer and fine raiment
he sets out to meet the great company of the dead.

At Halstatt, in the Austrian Tyrol, a great cemetery
of the Iron Age was discovered. This discovery was of
such importance that the name of the site has been
adopted to designate the early stages of the Iron cultures
in Europe. In the necropolis of Halstatt there were
993 burials : 525 simple inhumations, 455 cremated
bodies, and 13 partially cremated. Ramsauer, an eye-
witness of the excavations, was struck by the curious
medley of inhumed and cremated burials. The richest
materials—amber, glass, ivory, and oriental gold-work—
were in all cases with the burnt remains. Personal
ornaments were very numerous. (Dottin, by the way,

records the singular fact that a skeleton in one of the so-called " Galatian " tombs at Laybach on the Danube had a ring of bronze wire in the nasal cavity.) The bodies were usually placed on an east-west alignment, extended on the back or side. Sometimes there were two bodies side by side, or superimposed, irrespective of sex. Burnt and unburnt bodies had been placed together in the same tomb. The partial cremations are exceedingly curious : portions of the dissected body appear to have been consumed by fire, while the remaining portions were absolutely untouched ; sometimes the torso was burnt, and sometimes the head.

Incomplete burials have been found in Bavaria. In some of these extraordinary cases, the skull, femurs, or bones of the trunk are missing ; and in others, the skeleton has been broken in pieces, and some of the long bones placed over those of the trunk or by the side of it. Very often, the skull was placed in the middle of the body. Some of the burials consisted only of the bones of the arms and thighs, crossed over each other ; and in one instance they found only the pelvis, with incinerated human bones near it, and a number of bronze ornaments.

In the second phase of the Halstattian period, it is no uncommon thing to find that the swords and spears in the graves are crumpled up or bent. Whether the violation of tombs was not unknown at this period, and the weapons were rendered unserviceable as a measure of precaution, or whether the practice was purely ritualistic, we cannot say.

The burial places of the ancient Gauls have yielded many fine specimens of ornaments : neck-rings of iron and torques of bronze, glass bracelets, coiled finger-rings, bangles, brooches, hollow gold ear-rings, chains, and the most ancient and primitive of all decorations— pierced shells. Morel, at Bergères-les-Vertus, found the skeletons of a man and woman, face to face, their wrists joined together by a single bronze ring.

Chariot burials were frequent in the Marne area.
They were not unknown in Britain. In the so-called
" King's Barrow " in the East Riding of Yorkshire, the
skeleton of an old man, with arms crossed on breast and
legs crossed over each other, lay between the iron rims
of two chariot wheels, and close by him were the remains
of two very small horses.

At the time of the Keltic predominance in Central
and Western Europe, the simultaneous burial of a man
and a woman in the same grave (which we have noted
already in the neolithic period) occurs with marked
frequency.

Moreau excavated no less than fifteen thousand graves
belonging to this period in the Marne district : he had
the good fortune to discover twenty-two cemeteries,
and in these he worked with indefatigable zeal for
sixteen years. Among his discoveries was a large, long
and narrow grave containing the remains of some two
hundred skeletons, but not a single skull. We know
that the Kelts were ardent head-hunters, and, as there
were many swords and spears mixed up with the bones,
we may suppose that the grave contained the bodies
of slain fighting men, buried, after decapitation by the
victors, in a common pit. Coffins with iron nails were
occasionally used. Tools make their appearance in
the late Keltic burials—iron shears, awls, hammers,
gouges, punches, files, and saws. Personal decoration
becomes increasingly heavy and elaborate. The woman
of Peyre-Haute, buried full-length in an oblong grave
walled by big stones, had a necklace of nine amber
beads, seventeen beads of glass and twelve of bronze,
four or five brooches, no fewer than twenty-six bracelets
on her right arm and eight on her left, and forty-six
conical bronze buttons, which had evidently secured a
long robe, reaching from her throat to her feet.

In dealing with the facts of prehistoric burial, I have

been compelled to treat the subject in a somewhat arbitrary fashion. The neolithic and protohistoric periods offer to the student of necrology an astonishing mass of detail and variety of practice. I have only been able to select a few examples which might illustrate the ordinary procedures, together with a few of the more exceptional and problematical cases.

It is clear that, from remote prehistoric times, men have been careful to protect and provide for their dead, giving them all that was necessary for the life beyond the grave. Although we have no direct evidence of the practice of burial before the Moustierian epoch, it must be recollected that our knowledge of early palæolithic man hardly extends beyond our knowledge of his flint implements. Those implements give evidence of a degree of culture at least equal to that of existing primitive races, with whom burial is an established custom. We might therefore be justified in assuming, from indirect evidence, that the men of Chellean times—of the lower palæolithic age—had reached a level of culture at which the practice of burial, and the belief in all that is implied by that practice, might be regarded as almost certainly in existence. If this assumption were correct, we should be able to claim for the rites of sepulture an antiquity of two or three hundred thousand years.

We are justified, at all events, in believing that faith in immortality must have been already fully developed in an age so distant that it lies far beyond the reach of calculation. Let it be remembered that the Moustierian people buried their dead and made provision for their needs in the after-life. Let it be remembered that the Moustierian represents a form of humanity more primitive and more brutish than that of any other extinct or existing race of which we have knowledge We shall then realise that the belief in immortality appears to be present, as a fully matured conviction, while humanity is yet in its earliest and lowest stages.

CHAPTER IV

THE HEATHEN IMMORTAL

Primitive burials—Burial customs in Africa—The Australian Aborigines—The Tasmanians—Borneo and the Islands of the Pacific—The Andaman Islanders, the Veddas, and the Todas —The Indians of North America.

PRIMITIVE BURIALS

WHETHER the heathen who bows down to wood and stone can be justly accused of blindness, or not, he certainly bows with profound conviction. He bows, be it noted, not to the wood and stone as such, but as the haunt or the embodiment of the ancestral ghost. The wood and stone are merely incidental ; they are reminders, places of rendezvous with the departed, or things informed by the spirits of the dead. As we have seen, the cult of the dead appears to be the basis upon which primitive man builds up his primitive religion.

The burial rites of uncivilised people throw much light on the funerary practices of prehistoric times. On this account alone they are of great interest. But they are of even greater interest as exhibiting the mentality of the savage and his attitude towards the immortal dead. We have already outlined the main ideas of primitive man in regard to the destiny of the soul, and we shall now turn to an examination of his burial customs with a general understanding of their significance. Here, as in our review of prehistoric burials, we have to make a selection. We are still concerned with the ancient and the primitive. In the next chapter, dealing with Osiris and the Egyptian other-world, we shall pass to the purely religious form of the cult of the dead.

It will be convenient to treat our subject under racial or geographical divisions. I have chosen, for the general purposes of this book, those regions and peoples concerning which we possess the fullest and most reliable documentation, and those observances which may be regarded as illustrative of the essentially primitive outlook. The subject of primitive burial is one of vast extent. I have endeavoured to avoid choosing such instances as might suggest a partiality for a particular kind of evidence ; and it has been my aim to compare diverse forms of burial practice rather than to seek for a common interpretation of the facts.

The term burial customs is here used to cover the rites of mourning, the rites of anniversary or other commemoration ; and the term burial, as previously, denotes any ceremonial method of disposing of a dead human body.

BURIAL CUSTOMS IN AFRICA

The skilled anthropologist is not necessarily the most ingratiating of men. He may be deficient both in tact and in sympathy. In that case, his work in the field can never give the best possible results. That is why the man with ready intuition and quick understanding, even if he has little science, so often gets a clearer view of the primitive mind than his more highly trained associates. If you are able to treat a native chieftain as one great man should treat another, if you can enter into the spirit of native ceremonial, and cut a few capers, or sing, if need be, you will gain the esteem and confidence of the community, and you will penetrate more deeply into the social atmosphere than you would if you maintained a scholarly aloofness.

The records of the earlier travellers have often a

peculiar vividness and value. They are the records, in
many cases, of unprejudiced personal observation, not
hampered by the desire to reconcile facts with theories.
Moreover, the earlier observers had a chance of studying
the character of primitive man before that character
was changed or tainted by intercourse with civilised
races.

Skertchly, whose excellent book on Dahomey was
published in 1874, was not a scientist. He went out to
instruct the king of Dahomey in the use of fire-arms.
But he was a man whose courage, geniality, and impressive bearing won the regard of the royal negro and his
courtiers ; and he was privileged, as the honoured guest
of the king, to witness the great commemorative rituals
known as the Attoh Custom and the So-sin Custom.
These rituals took place on alternate years at Abomey—
one year the So-sin and the next the Attoh. They were
instituted in order to preserve the memory of the
departed kings and to promote friendly relations
between the powerful living and the powerful dead.

On the occasion of the So-sin rites witnessed by
Skertchly, special huts and sheds were erected, and in
these were placed the men destined for sacrifice. Some
of the victims were bound to posts ; others, lashed on
stools or on the bamboo trays used for carrying loads,
swung beneath the rafters ; and most of them, it seems,
were " in the best of spirits." Twelve of them sat in a
sort of decorated barn : they were dressed in white
shirts with scarlet trimmings, and a red heart on the
left breast and right shoulder, and they wore long
pointed white caps on their heads. Above them, on
stools fastened to the roof-beams, were four others,
similarly dressed, but gagged ; these poor creatures
were unable to laugh and talk as the others did, but they
swayed their heads to the rhythm of the music—the
dismal music of harsh voices and of drums. All the
victims were criminals who had been previously sentenced

to death. There were about fifty of them. It appears, from the account of Edouard Foà (1895), that if a sufficient number of criminals was not available, strangers —never native Dahomeyans—were added to the list. In general, Skertchly's account is confirmed by Foà, but the latter describes the condition of the human victims (he is alluding in particular to those who were captured for the purpose) as piteous in the extreme.

On the first day of the rites, king Gelélé, accompanied by the unseen ghost of his father Gézu, visited the principal victim-shed. Stools and umbrellas were set up in front of the shed for the spirit of Gézu and for the Bush King—an entirely fictitious spiritual personage, invented by the monarch in order that he might be spared the ignominy of becoming a trader (all contracts were made in the name of the Bush King). Gelélé then poured out twenty-seven quarts of rum and gin as an offering to the illustrious ghost, whose health he proceeded to drink, screened by a cloth, and all present hiding their faces.

The second day was the day of fetching the ghost-water, which was ceremonially taken from the royal pit. On the third day the sacred Nunupweto cloth was unrolled, and men heard the ominous throbbing of the death-drum. The king changed his dress repeatedly, and danced to the ghost of his royal father (as the Egyptian king Semti danced before the god of the white crown, six thousand years ago). This dance was intended to win the favour of the ghost and to gain his assistance in war. The fourth day was called " The Officers will look at a Marvellous Sight." Skulls were displayed, and the king, after shaking hands with eight fetiche-women, who impersonated the eight royal ghosts of his line, flung handfuls of cowrie-shells to the nobles, to some of the victims, and finally to the mob behind the barriers. The fifth day was a day of dancing, and of working up war-like enthusiasm. The sixth day was

spent in quiet and fasting. At night, the king " in
fetiche dress" marched with his wives in torchlight
procession to the Uhunglo market : there he struck off
the head of a messenger, having charged him to tell
the shades of the kings that he was about to send
them their retinue. After this, a cat, an alligator, and
a hawk were dispatched in like fashion, so that they
might quickly carry the news to all birds, beasts, and
fishes. Then the human victims were killed by being
struck on the head with a heavy knobbed stick ; their
bodies, after a certain mutilation, were fixed in various
positions upon gallows. All this ghastly business was
purely ritualistic. The king took no delight in the
killing, and Skertchly says that he saw him " turn from
the execution scene with a shudder." The day following,
there were eighteen bodies in the market-place : some
hanging head downwards from the transverse bars of
the gibbets, others slung horizontally, others seated on
stools on the cross-beams, with their dunce's caps on
their heads. Before the Bo-so or fetiche altars in the
palace were twelve severed heads, planted face downwards in little mounds of earth. The final ceremony
lasted for sixteen hours (sorely trying the patience and
endurance of poor Skertchly), and in this occurred a
grand march-past of state dignitaries, hunters, warriors,
and fetiches. Among the persons and things which were
paraded were the ornaments destined for the decoration
of Gelélé's tomb, and a girl dressed in white who was to
receive his soul when it arrived in Deadland. In the
procession of the royal treasures came a great drum with
twenty-two human skulls fastened to it, followed by a
woman with an executioner's knife ; silver galleons, brass
pans full of skulls ; coaches, hammocks, a sedan chair
and a Bath chair, cannon, and many other curious and
valuable objects.

The Attoh or Platform Custom had also, as its main
purpose, the honouring and remembrance of the royal

shades. Certain details, which differ from those of the So-sin rites, are worthy of note.

The night before the beginning of the Attoh, a large platform was set up, with a shed on it for the housing of the victims. In the shed were placed twenty-six men, gagged, and bound in a sitting posture on basket-work trays. The sides of the platform and the roof of the shed were covered with white calico and decorated with guns and powder-kegs. Another structure near the fetiche house gave accommodation to sixty-two victims. The Attoh ceremonies lasted for eight days. Seven days were taken up with dances, executions, court affairs, religious processions and state parades. On the eighth day the king and his courtiers placed themselves on the platform, beneath which two executioners with their great knives, and four ceremonial flesh-eaters, took their position. The victims, in their trays, were carried to the parapet of the platform, one by one, and set before the king. For the space of a few seconds, the monarch gazed intently at the gagged and pinioned messenger ; then he gave a sign to the assistants, and the man was toppled over to his death. To the first messenger the king entrusted his greetings to the shade of his father, ending with " Go !—may god and the fetiche be with you : go ! "—he then touched him lightly with his finger, and in a few seconds the man's head was hacked from his body by the executioner (Foà). The succeeding messengers were merely asked if they understood what they were to say when they reached Deadland. Pieces of flesh were cut from one of the head-less bodies by the flesh-eaters, roasted, and paraded on skewers ; the actual eating was a pretence, the flesh being chewed and spat out, after which the eaters took a powerful emetic. Foà says that the decapitated bodies were buried in the woods, each with a bottle of tafia and some cowries ; but Skertchly tells us that he saw two Nago captives beheaded as advance messengers

on the day before the custom, and that their bodies
were flung into a ditch and subjected to every sort of
indignity.

Skertchly was allowed to visit the royal tombs. The
resting places of the first three kings of the empire were
low circular huts, surmounted by a domed thatch roof,
and above this were silver ornaments, crowned by a sort
of fixed weathercock. Around the tombs were mounds
of earth full of human skulls, and there were lesser
mounds which contained thigh-bones. Fetiches, placed
before the tombs, appear to have been associated with
the ghosts of the kings, and they were refreshed, at the
time of the rites, with basins of human blood and with
holy water. The ashes of four kings were contained
within " a long barn with a high-pitched roof." On
the ridge of the roof were four silver ornaments : one
for each king. In front was a heap of earth with skulls
on it, and piles of human bones were scattered here and
there on the ground. The spirit-house of the great king
Gézu was " an oblong edifice of twice the size of the spirit-
houses of the other kings." In it was a large brass
" apron " or screen, made of forty sheets of brass
hinged together, suspended by chains of flat brass plates
from an embossed ridge-piece of the same metal. Thirty-
seven bells were fastened to the lower edge of the screen,
and eighteen other bells depended from a horizontal
wheel above the ridge-piece. The tinkle of these bells
as they swung in the wind was recognised as the voice
of Gézu calling to his son.

As regards the burial of ordinary folk in Dahomey,
there were two separate rites : the actual burial (beneath
the floor of the house) and the celebration of the funeral,
which might be after an interval of a few days, or a
whole year later. In Ashanti, the interval between the
two rites was sometimes as much as three years.

The people of Ashanti smoked the corpse over a slow
fire for several days, treating it with aromatic herbs :

it was then pushed into a corner and completely ignored until the date appointed for the *funérailles*.

In Fanti, a funeral was an expensive affair, and often entailed the complete ruin of a family. The corpse lay in state under a silk umbrella, with food and drink on a table within his reach. Handsome gifts were presented, amid the beating of drums and the firing of muskets. The body was buried in the house, and gold dust and other valuable offerings were placed in the grave. At the end of a year or so, sheep and cattle were sacrificed in honour of the deceased, and this " tendance " might be continued for many years, even after the house had crumbled away or had been pulled down. When a notable person died, his slaves made off as fast as they could into the bush, to avoid being dispatched to look after the ghost. At the burial of a nobleman, the heads of human victims were placed in the bottom of the grave, and the coffin was lowered on top of them.

The funerals of negro chieftains were, in many cases, scenes of almost unimaginable horror. So great was the dread of the powerful ghost that instant steps were taken to counter any feelings of resentment or suspicion on his part. Poor mangled creatures were thrust, alive and suffering, into the burial pit, while others were put to death in the rooms or courtyard of the residence of the deceased, or in places which were familiar to him during his lifetime.

The roasted body of a Unyoro chief rested, in a deep and spacious grave, on the knees of his living wives. Amid a deafening and hideous uproar, the pit was then filled with unwilling victims, seized by the chief's body-guard, and earth was trampled down upon the writhing mass. At the death of a king of Karague, his body was sewn up in a cow-hide and floated in a boat on the lake, until it was in an advanced state of decomposition. It was then placed in a hut, together with five virgins and fifty cows; the hut was closed, and the living creatures left to die. The grave of a Manyema chief was floored with the bodies of ten living women ; on these the dead chief was laid, and ten men, their limbs, like those of the women, previously broken, were also cast into the pit. Gaga notables were buried sitting on a seat, accompanied by two wives, whose legs and arms were broken : the grave was then filled up, and saturated with oil and blood. The dead king of the Bakitara lay in his tomb on a bed of bark and cow-hides ; two of his widows lay on either side of him, covering themselves with bark-cloths : a loose pile of bark-cloths filled up the grave, and the women died, either of starvation or of suffocation (Roscoe).

In the Congo, a man will do much and sin much in order that he may secure the means of providing himself with a fine funeral. The preparations for this funeral may last for many months, while the body is kept drying in a pit. The face of the corpse is daubed with ochre and white clay, and, during the sitting in state, a tobacco pipe is pushed into the mouth.

Many of the details of African burial are too nauseating for inclusion here. One instance, however, of the absorption of the qualities of the deceased by the living, of the distribution of his vital essence through direct communion, should be noted. The Banzini place the dead body on a grid with a fire beneath it. As the melting fat drips from the corpse it is received in pots, and rubbed into the hands and faces of the mourners. The residue of this ointment is rinsed off with warm water, and the rinsings are drunk by the near relations. Pots of fat may be sent to friends who live at a distance. In this revolting practice (and we shall see variants of it elsewhere) we have what is, in the exact sense of the term, a form of mystic communion. It may be that the desire is to retain the vitality of the deceased for the benefit of the aggregate social vitality. It may be that such an act serves to lessen the sense of loss, and to compensate, in some way, for the withdrawal of the visible presence of the defunct. But, whatever the reason, it is an act which proves that the spiritual or vital essence is thought of as never wholly separated from the material body, or any part of it.

THE AUSTRALIAN ABORIGINES

Alike in mentality and structure the Australian native is the most primitive of existing types of man. According to Sir Arthur Keith, he may be singled out, from among all living races, as " the nearest approach to the living ancestor of modern mankind." The Tasmanian, now extinct, represented an even more ancient type (Boule). The native Australians are a people whose culture is that of a true Stone Age. At the same time, it cannot be said that their culture corresponds definitely to any one of the recognised palæolithic periods : the Australians produce simultaneously objects which are reminiscent of those produced at different and widely separated phases of the Old Stone Age in Europe.

A primitive people does not long survive the invasion of its territory by a civilised race. Civilisation, with strong liquors and deadly diseases, with its unchanging will to convert and appropriate, very soon alters, and finally destroys, the native race and character. The Australian black man is decreasing steadily in numbers. His extinction is only a matter of time. It is extremely fortunate, for us, that he has been studied by three men who were almost ideally qualified for their task—Spencer, Gillen, and Howitt.

The burial rites of the aborigines of Australia, particularly those of the Warramunga clan, have been closely and carefully observed, and in view of their extraordinary interest we must examine them in some detail.

Among the northern tribes, the body is either buried in the earth or placed in a tree ; or tree-burial may

precede earth-burial. The Arunta bury the body in a
sitting position, with the face turned towards the spirit-
home in the Alcheringa. In the tribes bordering the
Gulf of Carpentaria, the flesh of the dead is eaten.
Among the Unnatjera and Kaitish, aged people are
buried with scant ceremony ; but with the Dieri of
the Lake Eyre district, in the south, age commands
respect, and the greater the age the greater the respect.

The hideous mourning rites of the Warramunga have
already been described (p. 69), and it will be remembered
that the body was carried away and placed in a tree.
After the preliminary disposal of the corpse, the relatives
concern themselves with the question of vengeance,
for death is regarded as the outcome of evil spells.
First they visit the little mound which has been raised
over the spot on which the man died, to see if they can
find any clues. Then they visit the tree. Walking in
single file, stealthy and silent, they hope to surprise the
spirit of the murderer (the spirit of a living man) perched
up in the tree, gloating over his dismal work. If they
are not successful, the body is left on the tree-platform
until the liquids of putrefaction trickle down and flow
over the ground : if they flow far, the murderer belongs
to a distant clan ; he may be discovered in the form of
a little beetle called *teiri*, and if this is killed the murderer
perishes. But vengeance is not always so easily satisfied.

The tree is then abandoned for a year at least, during
which time the dead man's ghost hovers near the remains
of the body, and pays visits to the camp. Then come the
final rites. The bones are raked down from the platform
with a stick (no one may touch them with his hands),
and pushed into a dish of bark. One of the radii is set
aside on a strip of paper bark, and the skull is smashed
to bits. The dish of bones is carried to an ant-hill, the
top of which is removed, and the bones are slipped into
the centre of it. After that, the hill is made up again.
The arm-bone is then placed in a decorated bark case,

" a torpedo-shaped parcel eighteen inches long"
(Spencer and Gillen), and this is put in the hollow trunk
of a gum-tree. Next day, the camp prepares for the
bringing-in of the bone.

As a prelude to this extraordinary ceremony, the young
women, instructed by their elders, paint the upper part
of their bodies with red and yellow ochre. In the rites
actually witnessed by Spencer and Gillen the following
was the sequence of events : A group of silent men
and women waited with bowed heads. Then they saw
the three men who had taken the bones from the platform, walking towards them rapidly in single file, the
leader carrying the parcel in a wrapping of small boughs.
Twice they walked round the group ; then the bone
in its wrapping was placed on the knees of an old man,
and the three others took no further part in the ceremony.
After the bone had been handed over, the men bent
over it reverently, while kneeling women wailed and
howled. Nothing further was done with the bone for
seventeen days, but a series of drawings in connection
with a snake totem was being made, and it was decided
that the last funeral ceremony should take place at
the close of a special totem performance. A drawing
of the ancient snake was made on the ground, and close
to this they dug a little pit. Ten men were decorated
with red, white, and yellow down : a trench about one
foot deep and fifteen feet long was dug on the corrob-
boree ground, and the ten men straddled across it, their
hands clasped behind their heads. The other men sat
by the drawing, save one, who stood near the little
pit with a stone axe in his hand. At this stage, the
women appeared, an old one telling the others what to
do, and on approaching the trench they formed single
file, the one who came last carrying the arm-bone in
its wrapping (the *burumburu*). Then the women crawled
one after the other along the trench and between the
legs of the straddling men, afterwards forming a dense

group, with their backs to the men and their hands clasped behind their heads. As the last one came from under the men and rose to her feet, the *burumburu* was snatched from her by a brother of the deceased. He took it to the man with the stone axe, who now stood with his weapon uplifted and ready to strike. The bone was smashed with one blow, thrust in the pit, and covered with a flat stone. When the women (who were not allowed to look) heard the stroke of the axe, they ran with loud cries to their camp, and there made great lamentation. The spirit of the deceased, no larger than a grain of sand, was now free to return to its home in the Wingara and await rebirth. It should be noted that the funeral here described was that of a woman. (Among other tribes also, the arm-bones receive special treatment, and are the objects of elaborate ceremonial.)

The Gnanji believe that a woman has no soul. They place the corpses of their younger dead on tree-platforms, and, when most of the flesh has decayed, the bones are wrapped in paper bark and left for a while longer on the platform. When the bones are white and clean, the fibulæ are ochred and kept for magical purposes ; the clavicles and radii are sent to distant groups, to summon them to a ceremonial gathering, and the other bones are handed to the man who is to be the avenger. Finally, all the bones are buried in a bark wrapping.

After the death of a Binbinga man, his body is cut up by his fellows. They dismember and decapitate him, and remove his liver. The different parts are then cooked on heated stones, covered with green boughs and earth, and eaten. Much the same thing takes place in the Mara and Anula tribes.

Among these people, the avenging of a death, which may take place a year or more after the body has been eaten, is preceded by elaborate rituals. The bones of the defunct are preserved, and one of the arm-bones,

wrapped in fur-string and coated with pipeclay, is sent
with a messenger to summon the clans. The messenger is immune and sacred, and the power of the bone
which he carries is so great that no man may refuse
him. So the envoy returns with a large company, whose
approach is made known by smoke-signals. The centre
and director of the strange and complex ceremonies which
follow is the father, or a near relative, of the dead man.
On the fourth day of the ceremonies, which include the
placing of the bones (except the arm-bone) in the boughs
of a tree overhanging a water-hole, the avenging party
is organised. The organiser ties the decorated arm-
bone close to the stone head of his spear, and when the
deed is done, he brings back the spear and bone, all
bloody, to the father of the dead man, who unties the
bone and buries it with the others by the water-hole.
Extraordinary scenes are witnessed at the departure
and return of the avenging party. To attain its object,
such a party will cover considerable distances—a
hundred miles or more.

The Dieri live in the neighbourhood of Lake Eyre
in South-East Australia. When a Dieri man is at his
last gasp, the relatives form two groups, one close to
the moribund, and the other at some distance. The
people in the latter group are the grave-diggers ; they
take care not to see, or be seen by, the dying man.
When the body is prepared for burial, the big toes, and
sometimes the thumbs, are tied together. Wrapped up
in a rug or a mat, the corpse is carried to the graveside
on the heads of three or four men, and is there laid on
its back. After a pause of a few minutes, the bearers
kneel by the grave, and some other men place the corpse
on the heads of those who are kneeling. An old man
who is related to the deceased then takes two rods,
and holding one in each hand he knocks them together.
As he does this, he calls on the dead man to give them
the name of the person who has caused his death. But

as the corpse is not in a position to make reply, the men who are sitting round answer for him. The name of some unfortunate man (always a member of another group) is spoken, and at this the corpse is dropped from the heads of the bearers and falls into the grave. It is then covered by the leaves of a plant. Next, an old man steps down into the grave, and cuts away the fat from the face, arms, thighs, and stomach of the dead body ; and this is handed round to the relations, who swallow it. In this ghastly communion a form of etiquette is observed : the father does not eat of his children, neither do the children eat of their sire. Some of the other tribes consume the flesh also, and it is preserved in bags, to be chewed as a relief from sorrowful thoughts. A Dieri tomb is often carefully tended : food and drink are placed thereon, and in cold weather a fire is lighted to cheer the shivering ghost.

According to Howitt, the Yerkla-mining "never bury their dead or dispose of them in any way." The dying person is made comfortable, and the folk leave the neighbourhood. The sick and wounded are treated with kindness.

The Tongaranka have a curious ceremony. They place the body in a sitting position, and provide it with a number of useful things. Before the grave is filled up, the nearest male relation stands over it and is struck with a boomerang, so that his blood drips down on the dead man, who is doubtless greatly refreshed.

The Wiimbaio, now extinct, dared not look on the face of a dead person, and covered it quickly with a skin rug. It was well known among the Jupagalk people that, when a man died, the *gulkan-gulkan* or spectre of the person who had killed him would come spying about in the bush at twilight. The friends of the deceased would therefore steal out of the camp and watch for this furtive apparition. When they saw it, and recognised it, they banded themselves together for the purpose of stealthy vengeance, and killed the murderer.

Cremation was not unknown among the Victorian tribes. The body of a common person was often burnt when there was neither time nor occasion for making a proper grave. After the death of a chief, his arm and leg bones were removed, scraped clean with a flint knife and placed in a basket : the body was then bent up and wrapped in an opossum rug, and set on a stage in the fork of a tree, to be cremated after the expiry of one moon. The Port Jackson tribes used to bury young people, and burn those who were past middle age.

Primitive as they were, many of the Australian tribes had evolved a clearly defined aristocracy. At the death of a notable, there would be a general chopping and searing of heads and limbs ; but ordinary men were buried with little ceremony, and women (as a rule) with none at all. It was usually considered, among the Maranoa, that the body of one who had died a premature or violent death would not rest in its grave, and it was therefore dried and carried about for as long as three years. Anointing with the fat of the deceased, with the object of acquiring his virtues and courage, was a frequent practice among the south-eastern tribes ; a practice which was sometimes varied in a particularly horrible manner. Extreme fear of the dead prevailed among the Herbert River tribes : the dead body was severely beaten with clubs, and it was weighted with stones, pushed in through sundry incisions. Fear was also strongly apparent in the case of the Melville and Bathurst Islanders (who occasionally cooked and ate the dead), for they flung spears into the side of the grave and among the grave-posts, crying loudly and stamping their feet, in order that the ghost might be dissuaded, or prevented, from returning.

THE TASMANIANS

Without doubt the Tasmanians were the most primitive people existing in modern times. What we really know about them does not amount to much. They were exterminated like vermin (one cannot even say, like game), with guns, dogs, and poison, by the white settlers ; save a wretched remainder who perished in captivity. The last pure-blooded Tasmanian (a woman) died in 1876. Our information concerning this interesting and most ill-fated race is derived from a number of prejudiced and contradictory accounts, written by men who, for the most part, showed but little skill in their observation and but little accuracy in their writings. No other accounts of a savage people are more villainously sententious or more dismally disfigured by cant.

It is not easy to arrive at the facts concerning the burial customs and the beliefs of the Tasmanians. Péron, who visited the island some time before it was invaded, and its people destroyed by the settlers, gives a description of graves surmounted by structures of grass, bark, and boughs, and containing partly cremated remains. He says that the fragile tomb and its contents were soon swept away by wind and rain. Later writers tell us of burials upright in hollow tree-trunks, a spear driven through the neck of the corpse maintaining it in position. Others speak of inhumation, and of the provision of a spear, so that the dead man might be able to fight when he was " asleep." Backhouse gives an account of the complete incineration of a dead woman at the Flinders Island settlement. At the burning, all the sick people sat round about, for they believed—poor wretches—that the soul of the deceased would come and " take the devil out of them." But it was the white man's devil, and there was no ridding themselves of him. The ashes were collected in a kangaroo skin, and just before dawn every morning these ashes were rubbed over the faces of the survivors, who, with visible and poignant sorrow, intoned a death-song.

BORNEO AND THE ISLANDS OF THE PACIFIC

Throughout Indonesia and the scattered islands of the Pacific we find a great diversity of funeral practice, with a few more or less invariable features, such as the special treatment of the skull. A copious ethnographical literature, of unequal value, deals with the people of these islands. No one can refer to that literature without paying tribute to the consummate skill of Sir J. G. Frazer, though we should not forget that his brilliant and masterly compilations are only made possible through the labours of less illustrious but not less industrious men who have worked long and patiently in the field. In connection with Borneo, the name of Ling Roth must always be remembered. Indonesian cultures have been closely studied by W. J. Perry, and Melanesian society by W. H. R. Rivers.

The primitive character of a people is soon effaced, as we have observed, by contact with civilisation. In these Oceanic regions, as elsewhere, the scientist often arrives too late on the scene. He arrives after the agents of mercantile or imperial enterprise have done their worst, and he finds a people who have already been brought to a state of physical and moral decadence.

Cremation was practised by the Land Dyaks of the Sarawak area in Borneo. The Sikongs burnt the bodies of their chief men; those of inferior standing were buried; and those of the lowest social grade were merely rolled in mats and put out in the jungle. Among the Bombok Dyaks, only the undertaker was present when the body was cremated. Mr. Low, viewing the matter from the exalted standpoint of the superior white person, said that " death, to their ignorant and unenlightened minds, displays no terror." The Sea Dyaks disposed of the dead by earth-burial. As soon as death had occurred, the female relatives washed the body and dressed it in its finest garments ; and it was then rolled up in cloth or matting. Cemeteries always excited the fears of these people, and, when passing them, they would throw down some little offering which they regarded as pleasing to the shades of the dead. The Lundus, when they moved their camp, dug up the ancestral bones and carried them along : a custom which recalls that of the North American Indians. Graves were very shallow, because no one dared to get into them, and the depth was thus limited by the reach of the arm of a person lying on the brink. With the body were placed clothes, weapons, and musical instruments, according to the sex or proclivities of the deceased : some of these things were property and others were gifts. The grave was fenced round, food and drink were placed within the enclosure, and at each end was a symbol indicative of the sex or calling of the departed.

The Milanaus occasionally bound living slaves to stakes by the side of a tomb, and left them to die there. The Baran were careful not to hold back the valuables of the defunct ; they buried with him his skull-trophies and all his other treasures. Many of the Borneo tribes used to dress the dead man in all the finery that he possessed, and they would sit him up, with a cigar or cigarette stuck in his mouth, and talk to him in a cheerful and friendly manner. Often the deceased would take with him a supply of cigarettes for distribution among his relatives in the underworld : " these . . . retain the smell of the hands which made them, which the dead relations are able to recognise." Soul-boats were sometimes provided : either models set on the grave, or real boats, sent out to sea with property, or even a female slave, on board. Burial houses of elaborate structure, richly carved and decorated, were set up on wooden pillars. Slaves and followers were sacrificed, and the principal supporting-post of these houses was sometimes driven down through the living body of a captive.

The Barawans kept the dead, encased in highly embellished coffins, in their houses for several months. The coffins were made air-tight with a resinous stuff, and bamboo pipes were carried from them into the ground beneath. Hurricane lamps and bottles of paraffin were among the things which were considered useful for the ghost.

Jar-burial was in vogue in certain parts of Borneo. Usually the body was doubled up and forced into the jar, which was then closed with a piece of hide and sealed with gum : after being kept in the house for some days it was buried. The Murut people broke the jar, and then built it up round the body, holding it together with cement, and securing the top by a cemented plate. A bamboo drain was conducted from the bottom of the jar to the ground, and the whole thing was kept in the house for a year. At the end of that time, the dry bones were placed in a smaller vessel, and buried with rejoicing. In other cases, the bones were deposited, after the decay of the flesh, in a burial urn ; and in others, the partly decomposed body was squeezed into the jar.

Captives were ceremonially killed in Borneo, as in Africa, so that they might carry messages to the dead. These captives were bought by a number of subscribers, all of whom, when they were dispatching a messenger, grasped one long spear and gave their messages as they slowly pushed it into his body. A variant of this unpleasant procedure consisted of a gradual stabbing to death.

In Dutch Borneo, cremation seems to have been the final stage ; regarded as an act of purification and cleansing from sin. Burial places were generally on a hill or rising ground, overshadowed by trees. Before digging a grave, a fowl was sacrificed, to propitiate the shades, who might otherwise look on the new corpse as an intruder who had not paid his way. The bodies of medicinemen were suspended from trees in the cemetery. A festival of the dead was held, but not at fixed periods. For the convenience of the invited ghosts a toy boat was dispatched, but its ghost-counterpart was a mighty war vessel, hailed by the shades with cries of joy. The motives for the festival appear to have been two : (a) the enjoyment of a good feed, (b) the final severance of all ties between the ghosts and the living. In ancient times, the provision of a fresh human head was an essential.

As regards head-hunting, a custom often allied to funeral practices, it seems that the main idea was that the souls of those whose heads had been obtained by the Dyak during his lifetime would be his servants in the world of shades. Heads were also propitiatory offerings to the angry dead, proofs of manliness, offerings to the spirits of fertility (that is, to the dead in another form), and acceptable presents for women. Crossland saw women, when a head was given to them, " kiss it, bite it, and put food in its mouth."

We will turn to the burial customs of the Melanesian folk.

Surely the strangest of all funeral rites are those of the Solomon Islanders, and particularly of those who live on the island of Rauro or San Cristoval. According to Dr. C. E. Fox, these folk have no fewer than twentyone different ways of disposing of their dead. The more exceptional of these ways are, burial in the ground upright ; in " a cave cut in a living tree " ; in a large bag, sitting ; squatting above ground by the side of a tree ; burial in a food bowl, and burial in the sea. Cremation and embalming are practised to a certain extent. They also build a tomb which resembles the

Egyptian *mastaba* (to be described later), with a stone skull-house of dolmen type on the top of it, a shaft, and a chamber. But to suppose that there is a link between the culture of these people and the culture of the ancient Egyptians is a learned absurdity which does not survive critical examination.

The sea-burials of San Cristoval are exceedingly weird and strange. You look down on a white sandy floor, through water of translucent green, and there you see the dead. Some are standing, others are sitting, others lying on their backs. Their positions are maintained by weights. Those who are standing have branches tied to their hands, so that the body sways to and fro in the tide-stream and the arms move gently this way and that way. After the body has been sunk, the male relatives dive down after it and arrange it in position. We are told by Rivers that the natives of Duke of York Island used to throw corpses into the sea with weighted feet, so that they assumed an upright position in the water.

Preservation of skulls in models of fishes, in shrines or in boxes, is a marked feature of the cult of the dead in the Solomon Islands.

In the Torres Straits Islands there are dances and masques of death, in which the deceased, the messenger of death, and companies of ghosts are impersonated by the actors. A rough and ready sort of mummification is sometimes practised, and the dried body, swaying and rustling in the wind like a bunch of desiccated sea-weed, dangles from the centre of the hut.

The notable feature in the funeral customs of New Guinea is the removal and preservation of the bones. If it is not buried, the body is made up into a bundle and left above ground.

In some of the Banks Islands the body was " dried over a slow fire for ten days or more " (Frazer), and the women watchers drank the juices of decomposition.

The Tongans, a remarkably fine race, used to bury their chiefs in great stone chambers. Burial in the earth was almost invariable, and the body was laid at full length. The mausoleum of an important family consisted of a dolmenic chamber in its most colossal form ; the floor, each side, and the roof of the chamber were single blocks of stone ; and the covering slab was often so massive that two hundred men were required to move it.

In the Hervey Islands, the dead body was finely decorated, and a baked pig, with vegetables, laid upon it. Big stones were piled on the grave to prevent the ghost (or the body animated by the ghost—probably, I think, the real idea in all such cases) from getting out.

Society Islanders crudely mummified the corpses of their noblemen and placed them in mortuary lodges, where they received offerings and listened to pious lamentations. When the flesh had gone, the skulls were removed, and preserved by the families to which they belonged. In war-time, the enemy would sometimes ransack these mortuaries and get hold of the bones, which they made gleefully into hooks and other implements—truly a "tragical abomination." To avoid this indignity, the bones were hurriedly removed, if there was sufficient warning, and placed in wellnigh inaccessible caves in the mountains. Precautions of an obviously hygienic nature were observed in the case of any one who died of an infectious disorder, and in general the contagion of death was greatly feared.

In Samoa, the body of a dead chief was often carried round to all the places with which he was familiar in his lifetime. "The various modes of preservation of the bodies of the dead all seem to imply the absence of any special fear of the dead ; or if such fear be present, we must regard preservation as part of a cult whereby the dead are rendered harmless, or even friendly " (Rivers).

The Marquesans were once " the noblest specimens

of the Polynesian race " (Frazer). Herman Melville, the author of *Moby Dick*, observed that the men were seldom under six feet in height. They thought that by bestowing the name of a dead person on any object they put that object under the immediate protection of the ghost. They had no fear of death (one of the advantages, presumably, of the " ignorant and unenlightened mind " of the heathen), and the Marquesan, when he felt that his demise was near, calmly ordered his coffin. The body of a chief, richly bedecked, might be kept for several weeks in the house, with his weapons and the skulls of his enemies by his side. As in the Society Islands, hostile invaders always tried to get the remains of the dead. Two or three people were sometimes slain to form the ghost-retinue of notables. The body of a great man was occasionally flayed, so that he might appear before the underworld gods without speck or blemish. The fear of ghosts was exceedingly strong, and no one dared to sleep in the house in which a person had died : in consequence of this, a dying man was generally accommodated with a little hut for himself, which, after his death, was destroyed.

For the most part, Micronesians are a jolly, chivalrous, and intelligent people. They are not quarrelsome or bloodthirsty : they are peaceable and fond of fun. But with them also, the fear of the dead is strong ; so strong that it breaks through their natural equanimity. On the three nights following a death, the Gilbert Islanders drove the ghost from the village, with a whirring and swishing of sticks and leaves, all threshing and beating away without a single word, and disbanding in silence. After the final drive on the third night, a woman, who was called " Lifter of the Head," placed the dead man's head in her lap, and recited the spells which sped the ghost on its journey.

Social distinctions were rigorously observed in the Marshall Islands. Chiefs were buried with appropriate ceremony, and their spirits were dreaded; but commoners, being of no account either in this world or the next, were pushed into the ground with callous indifference. The same sharp distinction was observed by the Ponapeans, and it is, indeed, common throughout Oceania.

Those remarkable folk, the Yap Islanders, had various forms of burial. If the deceased had died of sickness or mere decay he was buried with his knees drawn up; if he was killed in the wars, he was laid out straight; if a cough finished him, his head was bent down over his chest. A dead chief was clad in his best clothes, rubbed with oil, and tied to a scaffold in a sitting posture. His son placed a spear in the lifeless hand, and sat down opposite the body, chanting the virtues and notable deeds of the departed. In the interludes of the recital, mourners danced and wailed, receiving gifts from the dead man's son; and this went on day and night, the son fasting, and rarely quitting his station until the corpse fell to pieces. The remains were wrapped in fine mats and buried under a cairn on the hill-side; near this cairn the son built a hut of leaves, and there he remained in solitude for a hundred days. Similar piety on the part of the children of the deceased was found among the Pelew Islanders—a people whose religious history has been spoken of in our second chapter. The eyes of the corpse were closed by his sister, a small hut was built over the grave, and in it one of the children kept vigil, sitting in the light of an oil lamp, for several nights. Food was brought to the watcher, who buried some of it in the grave, and poured out drink. Over the burial place of a chieftain a much larger hut was built, and in this his female relatives lived for several days. The house of the deceased was tabooed. On the third day of the mourning, a heap of raw taro was piled in front of the door for the ghost to feed upon, and after this was removed a woman went into the wood and picked a bunch of flowers. After the evening meal another woman took the nosegay in a plaited sheath, while the chief mourner invoked the ghost, asking him to indicate the cause of his death. At the mention of the true cause, the flowers shook and fell to the ground. Next day, the nosegay, tied to a bamboo, was set up at the head of the grave, and the ghost was seen drawing near to it ; but it was carried off (we are not told how) by " the hostile deity who killed the sick man " (Frazer).

THE ANDAMAN ISLANDERS, THE VEDDAS, AND THE TODAS

We will now examine three groups which exhibit an extremely low mentality, only some degrees less primitive than the Australians—the one living in the Andaman Islands, two hundred miles south-west of the Irrawaddy delta, the other in Ceylon, and the third on the hills of Southern India.

The Andaman Islanders are a negrito people, formerly regarded as a fierce, anthropophagous folk. Early navigators gave the islands a wide berth, fearing lest, if shipwrecked thereon, they should be knocked on the head and put into the cook-pot. Of late years their numbers have decreased : civilised men have introduced syphilis and measles, and the islanders are now faced with slow extermination. When a death occurs, the camp is deserted for several months. There are no actual chiefs, but seniority is respected ; men who possess certain personal qualities are admired, and have considerable influence. It does not appear, however, that such men are buried with any special marks of distinction.

The news of a death spreads quickly. Women prepare the body for burial : the limbs are violently flexed, and a knife (formerly a shell with a sharp edge) is placed in the clenched fist of the corpse. A sleeping-mat is wrapped round the body, and a compact bundle is made by swathings of palm leaves bound with rope. Before the package is tied up, the relatives bid farewell by blowing gently on the face of the dead man. The women take no part in the actual burial. Those who die in the prime of life are honoured by having their remains placed on a tree platform, while immature or aged persons are put in the ground, in a hole three or four feet deep. In the case of earth-burial, the body is placed on its side, facing east (see p. 52). The head is supported on a wooden pillow, and a log on either side of the body keeps it in a comfortable position. After the earth has been shovelled in, a fire is lighted on the grave, and a bowl of water is provided. In platform-burial, the body lies sideways, facing east, and fire and water are placed beneath the tree. Whichever form of burial is adopted, plumes of shredded palm leaf, mounted on sticks or branches, mark the grave, so that no one may come on it unawares, disturbing the ghost. Signals of a like sort are set up at the entrance to the abandoned camp. But when children die, the camp is not abandoned, and the body, in the contracted posture, is buried beneath the family hearth. No respect is shown to the body of a stranger, which, among the northern tribes, was cut up and burnt. The blood and fat of the stranger (they said) flew up into the sky, and as the ghost was presumably drawn up after them, danger was averted. If possible, the body is buried on the day on which it dies, and if this cannot be done, all the camp keeps awake, the relatives sitting round the corpse, wailing and chanting.

The Veddas had no regular form of burial. They used to abandon the body in the cave or beneath the rock-shelter where death had taken place ; sometimes with a big stone on its chest, to keep it quiet, but usually they paid it no attention. Yet they had a strong desire to remain on good terms with their dead. Evident fear and evident affection ruled their attitude towards the deceased, but for his body or bones they had no respect whatsoever. There is no such thing, properly speaking, as Vedda burial. White men insisted on the decent interment of the Veddas, but the Veddas would exhume cheerfully any of their fellows for the benefit of the European scientist, or any other inquisitive person. No articles of property were ever left with a dead body : a man's belongings, however, were ceremonially purified after his death.

An important element of primitive psychology appears, therefore, to have been absent in the case of the Veddas. For them, the dead human body did not possess the tremendous significance which it has for most primitives : it did not possess any significance at all. At the same time, although no Vedda had ever seen one, they were convinced of the existence of ghosts and regarded them as extremely powerful. I have previously quoted Seligmann's affirmation that the Vedda religion is " essentially a cult of the dead." It is a cult in which the relics of the deceased play no part—they are, indeed, flung away carelessly, as things having neither value nor virtue.

The Toda funeral customs are complicated, and extend over a lengthy period.

An essentially pastoral people, the Todas are habitu- ally occupied with their buffaloes and dairies ; and as these things are of the greatest importance to the living it is not surprising to find that they are closely associated with the rites of the tomb. In some of the villages there are dairies which are used as mortuary chambers, and the hut in which the dead body is placed before its cremation, and in which the burnt relics are deposited prior to the second ceremony, is called *pali* or dairy.

The funeral rites take place within a stone circle, and the ashes are finally buried at the entrance to a ring of stones. There are special funeral grounds for men and

for women. Funerals may only take place on certain
days. When it is supposed that a man is dying, he is
dressed in all the finery that can be found in his house.
After death, the body is wrapped in a cloth, and then in
two mantles : it is carried to the appointed place on a
wooden bier, and must be taken by a prescribed route.
At the funeral ground, the body lies in state, while the
villagers, one by one, come up and bow reverently
before it, touching it with their foreheads. Then the
body is placed in the hut which has been built for it,
the women make a sound of mourning, and the men
prepare for the cremation.

Formerly, a Toda funeral was accompanied by a
great slaughter of buffaloes, which were penned within
a stone enclosure on the funeral ground. But the
British Government, distressed by what seemed to be
a foolish waste of live-stock, gave orders that the sacrifice
was not to exceed two buffaloes per funeral : apparently
one for the first ceremony and one for the second. The
selected animal is chased, seized, and thrown—a very
exciting scene—and felled by a blow on the head from
the back of an axe. As soon as the buffalo has been
brought down and is dying, the corpse is taken out of
the hut and placed near its head. " At the funeral of
a man, the covering of the body is unfolded and the
right hand of the dead man is made to clasp one of the
horns. At the funeral of a woman, the body is laid with
its feet by the mouth of the buffalo " (Rivers). Now
comes a very strange part of the ritual : the men salute
the buffalo by placing their foreheads on the horns and
on the head between the horns. The people then
gather round the body of the man and the body of the
animal, with loud lamentation. There is evidently
some mystic association between the buffalo and the
deceased, but the nature of this was not clear to Rivers.
After a rite known as the " cloth putting ceremony,"
in which women related to the corpse by marriage touch

it in turn with a bit of cloth, the burning of the body takes place.

The body is first laid on the bier and set down by the side of the pyre. Food and various small luxuries, with money and ornaments, are then stuffed into the large pocket of the cloak in which the body is wrapped, pushed among the folds of the cloak, and put in a brass bowl, or rattan boxes. The pyre is so constructed that it burns slowly, and after it has been lit, the body on the bier is lifted and swung three times over it, and then set down again. This serves at least one practical purpose. As the bier swings over the fire the soul of the deceased flits off to the other world, taking with it all the good things which have been so generously provided. But the mere substances of these things still remain, and as they are of no consequence to the ghost, the donors take them back—nay, they will even remove the bangles from the dead man's arms and the rings from his fingers. The ghost is the gainer, and yet the living lose nothing. After the cremation a piece of the skull is taken from the ashes, and this, with a lock of hair previously cut off, is retained for the second ceremonial. The ashes are left on the ground.

During the interval between the two ceremonies, (some days, weeks, or months, according to circumstances) the relics of the defunct are saluted by those of his village who were unable to attend the funeral. The second ceremony was a great event in the old days, but now, with the governmental restriction on the sacrifice of buffaloes, it has lost much of its glory and excitement. However, the Todas wait until a number of families are ready for the final ritual, and then they join forces ; so the show of buffaloes is not so bad. When these combined funerals take place, there is a hut for each individual set of relics. Although the ghost has left some time before (when the body was swung over the fire), he does not acquire his proper status in the

other world until the last rites have been duly performed. Sacrificial blood and sacred bark are scattered
about, and a young calf is ceremonially driven off the
ground. A buffalo is killed, food is distributed, there is
a dance, and then most of the people go home ; but a few
remain on the ground until the following morning.

The final rites are performed at a small circle of stones
called the *azaram*. The relics, and the objects to be
burnt with them, are brought from the hut and set near
the circle. Outside the circle a fire, fed by clarified
butter, consumes (if it is a man's funeral) a milk bowl
and a pair of imitation buffalo horns ; and then the
human relics are anointed with butter. A second fire
is now started inside the circle, and when the rites are
those of a combined funeral for persons of the same sex
and clan, all the relics are burnt together. With the
body of a male they burn supplies of food, money, clubs
and sticks, a basket, bow and arrows, a knife, the axe
used in felling the buffaloes, a palm-leaf umbrella,
and a special kind of sieve. As soon as the things are
in the fire, the *irsankâti* rite begins : a male cousin of
the dead man puts on certain female ornaments and
stands at the opening of the circle with his right arm
outside his cloak ; the man who has lit the fire comes to
his side, and the two stand together, crying loudly,
until the fire is out. At the funeral of a woman this
ceremony is performed by two women. Eventually,
the ashes are swept into a hole which has been dug at
the opening of the circle and covered by a stone. If
the funeral was that of a man, a bell-ringer now walks
three times round the burial place, while another man
holds his waist. Then the bell-ringer smashes a new pot
on the stone which covers the ashes ; he bows down,
touching the stone with his forehead ; gets up, and goes
to the funeral hut without looking behind him. This
action is repeated by the others, and the rites end with
the taking of food.

I have gathered these particulars from W. H. R. Rivers's book on the Todas, and I have given them somewhat fully because they are of special interest and significance.

THE INDIANS OF NORTH AMERICA

The American Redskins, while retaining many of the attributes of a very primitive race, had, at the time of their discovery by white men, reached a moderately advanced phase of material progress. Physically they were a fine people, and their character was marked by nobility, generosity, and courage. It is true that they were cruel and fiercely vindictive when hard pressed by the invaders : such propensities, however, are commonly developed by invasion, and are not peculiar to savages. Their burial customs—those of a highly organised primitive society—are extremely interesting.

With them, as with many other races, widely separated from them in every sense of the word, second burial was a very frequent practice. Months, even years, might elapse between the death and the final rites. Presents were often brought to the dying man (notably among the Algonquian tribes), so that the ghost, at the moment of its liberation, might be in a good humour.

Indian graves were often richly furnished, and the most highly prized objects were not withheld from their rightful owners. So it was, that the later burials contained many things of European make. On Rhode Island, people were buried with copper kettles pushed over their heads ; they had gunlocks, brassware, and scraps of military uniform.

One Captain Smith wrote concerning the Powhatans in 1612 : " But their chief God they worship is the Divell. Him they call Oke and serve him more of feare than love." Oke appears to be the god of the dead. Smith thus describes the preparation of the body for burial : " Their bodies are first bowelled, then dryed upon hurdles till they bee verie dry, and so about the most of their jointes and neck they hang bracelets and chaines of copper . . . their inwards they stuffe with copper beads and cover with a skin, hatchets, and such trash. Then lap they them very carefully in white skins, and so rowle them in mats for their winding sheetes." And a somewhat earlier observer, John White, a member of Raleigh's second expedition, wrote beneath his picture of the " Tombe of the Cherounes " : " . . . their flesh clene taken of from the bones save the skynn and heare of their heads, wch flesh is dried and enfolded in matts laide at their feete . . . with their Kywash, which is an Image of woode keeping the deade." Father Le Jeune, writing in 1636, says that the Hurons flexed the carcase as soon as it was dead, and that burial took place three days later. According to Lawson (1701) the Monacans laid the dead body on a piece of bark and exposed it to the sun, afterwards embalming it with a powdered root and oil : after further exposure on a platform, the flesh was scraped from the bones and the latter were oiled and put into a box.

Stone-lined graves, or kists, " small excavations . . . lined or partly lined with natural slabs of stone " (D. I. Bushnell), were very numerous in parts of the Mississippi Valley. Some of these were found to contain extended skeletons, and others a bundle of bones with the skull in the middle. In certain small kists were the bones of small birds and animals, and no trace of any human remains. A single mound might contain as many as a hundred burials ; the lower ones in square kists, and the upper ones in oblong kists, made to fit the extended body. Incomplete skeletons, mixed and broken bones, found in the smaller chambers, recall the neolithic tombs of Europe. A most peculiar wheel-like disposition was discovered in one of the tumuli : in the middle stood a sacrificial urn, and radiating from it, heads inward, like the spokes of a wheel, were a number of extended burials, while the rim or tyre was represented by an outer circle.

The Illinois tribes were still making stone-lined graves in the latter half of the eighteenth century. One of their burial mounds contained a rectangular chamber of logs and boulders, wherein were eleven skeletons sitting with their backs to the wall, and in front of them was a handsome drinking-bowl made of shell and surrounded by sherds of pottery. On two sides of this chamber were narrow cells, filled with a fine chocolate-coloured powder which " gave out such a sickening odour that it was found necessary to suspend operations until the next day " (D. I. Bushnell). The nature of this peculiar powder was not determined, though an analysis would surely have been an easy matter.

At the Huron feast of the dead, the bones in the cemeteries were reverently disinterred and buried in a common grave, together with the bodies of the recently deceased. The great burial pit was carpeted with new bear-skins. First, the entire bodies were laid gently down, and above these were deposited the bundles of clean bones.

Cairn burial—the piling of stones over a body or bodies lying on the surface of the ground—was practised by the Cherokees. The contents of a barrow in Tennessee were remarkable : there were thirteen complete skeletons laid out at full length, one with the arms extended horizontally ; a group of twelve skulls, not associated with any other remains, and all touching each other ; twelve more skulls in a round enclosure, resting, with some other bones, on a layer of coal and ashes ; and five skulls in the midst of a pile of mixed bones.

The Choctaw kept the body on a platform until it was highly putrescent, when the flesh was scraped away, and the bones, in a casket, were placed in the bone-house. When the house was full, the remains of the dead were carried by their respective families to a chosen

place, and there piled up in a heap and covered with
earth. Some say, that old men with long sharp finger-
nails used to remove the flesh of the corpse ; and others,
that the undertaker was a woman. The flesh was burnt,
buried, or merely thrown away. Here, as in so many
other cases, the final virtues and essence of the deceased
resided in his bones. The Chickasaw buried the dead
beneath the floors of their huts, but they were not in
the least incommoded by this grim proximity. Burial
beneath the floor was a custom of the Creek Indians
likewise : the dead man sat up in a deep cavity, and
with him were his bow and arrows, his musket, tobacco-
pipe, and club. He had also a supply of powder and
balls, of tobacco, and of vermilion. Creek burials,
however, show great diversity. Sometimes the grave
contains entire skeletons, sometimes only parts of skeletons or masses of bones, and sometimes the remains are
cremated—the ashes loosely strewn about, or enclosed
in urns.

The examples we have considered, taken from different
levels of primitive culture, illustrate more fully the
general ideas which were outlined in the first and second
chapters of this book. It would seem that the fear of
the dead, varying in intensity from mere misgiving to
abject terror, is a constant factor in the sum of the
primitive mentality. Affection for the dead is a variable
factor, and it does not appear to exist apart from a
general sentiment of which the marked characteristic
is fear. The body, and its separate parts, or any substances derived from it, are usually looked on as more
than symbolic of the spirit or of the personal essence ;
they are looked on as tangible forms of the spirit or of
the personality, by virtue of some mysterious process
of identification.

The rites of burial, therefore, are not by any means
simple in origin or intention. They are dictated by the

desire to accommodate several purposes; and those purposes seem often to be at variance with each other, or to be inspired by contradictory ideas. The spirit is in the tomb, but also in the underworld; it is free, but yet attached to the body or to the parts of the body. Hence it is, that the tomb may be at once a residence, a prison, and a meeting-place. The dead are honoured, and at the same time kept under restraint, by the contrivances of burial. Inconsistency of thought is not only compatible with absolute conviction, but seems, indeed, to be an inseparable part of it. For primitive conviction is certainly absolute; it does not admit the possibility of doubt. Whether a man has one soul or several, his personality, far from being extinguished by death, emerges from the sepulchre in a new, powerful, and terrible form.

The primitive notion of immortality implies no feeble or flimsy state of being, but a vigorous and mischievous existence. This notion sometimes reacts on primitive society in the most disastrous manner, involving sacrifice and cruelty as the proper means of appeasing the ghost.

In some cases, the ability of the ghost to visit, or remain in, his earthly haunts seems to be limited; in others, he is more or less permanently in touch with the earth, and free to return to it whenever he is in the mood to do so. However that may be, the fact which mainly concerns us is, that, in his primitive state, man does not question the survival of the human spirit. The cult of the dead passes from its stark, uncompromising aspect, and through the vaguer but more beautiful forms of a true religion, before it is faced, as all religions are faced in time, by the open defiance or the dull indifference, and the apparent immunity, of the unbeliever.

CHAPTER V

OSIRIS

The story of Osiris—The Egyptian doctrines in regard to the soul—The cult of Osiris—Predynastic and dynastic burials in Egypt.

THE STORY OF OSIRIS

TO the pious Egyptian, for some four thousand years, Asar, or Osiris, was " King of eternity, the prince of gods and men, god of gods, king of kings, governor of the world, whose life is everlasting." Austere yet just, terrible yet beautiful, his godhead was always dominant in the religious history of Egypt. He was regarded as the god who was once a man. As man and as god he overcame the power of death and darkness and promised a happy immortality to those who led righteous lives upon the earth. He symbolised family affection and the dues of kinship. He was the saviour of men, rewarding the godly and punishing the wicked. Above all, he was the lord of the dead, the president god of the other world, the judge of all human souls.

The legend of Osiris appears in its most complete form in the summary of Plutarch. According to this legend, Osiris was one of the children of Keb and Nut, primeval deities, and the brother of Horus the elder, of the arch-villain Set, and of Isis and Nephthys. He married Isis, his sister, and became king of Egypt. Devoted to the care and improvement of mankind, he desired to widen his beneficent reign until it should embrace all men and all countries. To achieve this aim, the royal philanthropist set forth on his travels, entrusting his kingdom to Isis. The queen, in her lord's absence, was exposed to the unwelcome attentions of Set (Typhon), who was her brother-in-law and brother. Set was repulsed, but he planned vengeance. With the aid of conspirators, he seized Osiris on his return and shut him in a wooden box, sealed with molten lead. The box was carried to the Nile and launched on its waters. Ultimately it was cast ashore at Byblos, and, as it grounded, a miraculous tree sprang up, enfolding the coffin in its substance. The rulers of Byblos were king Melkarth and queen Astarte. The king chose for one of the pillars of his palace that very tree which contained Osiris in his coffin ; and soon afterwards, the disconsolate Isis, looking for the body of her lord, entered the palace and spoke with the queen's tire-women. A strange delicious odour emanated from the person of Isis, and this was soon perceived by Astarte. Isis became nurse to one of the baby princes. As she nursed the child, she gave him her finger to suck, and at night she plunged him in the fire, so that his earthly parts might be consumed and he might acquire immortality ; while she, in the form of a swallow, flew round the pillar with sad twittering. One night, the queen saw the baby in the fire, snatched him out, and demanded an explanation from Isis. The coffin was taken out of the pillar and given to the goddess, who threw herself upon it with so terrible a cry that the king's youngest son died of fright. Taking the box, and the eldest son of king Melkarth, Isis entered a ship and set sail for Egypt. On the voyage, she opened the coffin and flung her arms about the dead body ; but when the king's son approached, she turned on him a glance of divine anger, and he, like his brother, fell dead through fear.

When she had returned to her kingdom, Isis put the coffin in a secluded place. Set, while hunting by moonlight, discovered it ; whereat he savagely cut up and mutilated the body, scattering it in fourteen portions throughout the land. Isis found all the portions, save one, and raised a monument over each of them.

Now we come to the difficult question of the begetting of Horus the younger. According to the Plutarchian version, Isis gave birth to Horus in a papyrus swamp, soon after the death of Osiris, and before the excursion to Byblos. But other accounts have it, that Horus was miraculously begotten by Osiris after his death. Be that as it may, Osiris, restored from the dead, found in his son Horus a ready and powerful avenger. The battle between Set and Horus lasted for several days ; Set was overcome, and led, a captive in fetters, to Isis, who, acting on a truly womanly impulse, gave him his liberty. Horus, raging, tore the royal crown from his mother's head, and she was given an ox-head crown by the god Thoth. Playing up to his part of the implacable villain, Set proclaimed Horus a bastard, but the case was brought before a court of the assembled gods, and the charge was refuted.

The legend is essentially the story of the good man, the faithful wife, the dutiful son, and the unrepentant scoundrel. As in many other primitive legends, the elements of the mortal and the divine are somewhat confused ; but, although Osiris was of divine parentage, he was certainly regarded as a man when he ruled over his earthly kingdom. It is a story which has always commended itself, in one form or another, to proper-minded and orderly people. It shows the family, sorely tried, but loyal and ultimately triumphant, defying the powers of evil. It shows love (legitimate love) victorious, and unity restored. That the marriage of a brother and sister is wicked, is an argument which has no place in mythologies : indeed, the marriages of the earlier gods were necessarily incestuous.

Set was quite alone in his villainy. He had married Nephthys, his own sister and the sister of Isis, but his wife loved Isis and did all that she could to help her. The

son of Set and Nephthys was Anpu (Anubis), the magician, who assisted Horus in bringing about the revival of
his father. In the later texts, the four sons of Horus are
assistants at the resurrection of Osiris. The chronology
of the legend is no doubt seriously disturbed by this,
as it was previously disturbed by the sudden growth of
Horus the younger, but such discrepancies are common
to all legends. Probably the Plutarchian version contains episodes and details which were not present in the
earlier forms of the story.

In any of its forms, the story is one calculated to make
the figures of Osiris and Isis exceedingly popular. It
was natural that the good man who became divine,
who vanquished the terrors of death, should be appointed the judge and ruler of the dead. Natural, also,
that the two women who loved and helped him should
stand beside his throne.

" The idea of the god-man Osiris," says Sir Wallis
Budge, " was developed naturally from the cult of the
ancestor." Whether the god Osiris was directly evolved
from a single human prototype, or whether he represents
the final outcome of the cult of ancestors, there is no
doubt whatever that his worship contains all the
elements of the primitive worship of the dead. Osiris
absorbed the attributes of the earlier gods, and survived
the passing sovereignty of usurping deities. He, the
great ancestor, the good king, the righteous judge of
the dead, had an assured place in the religion of Egypt,
and that place he held until Egypt was invaded by an
alien people with alien creeds.

THE EGYPTIAN DOCTRINES IN REGARD
TO THE SOUL

The belief of the ancient Egyptians concerning the
nature and existence of the physical and spiritual parts
of the human personality is, in its fully developed form,

exceedingly complex. According to their doctrines, the
personality consists of several distinct parts, to some
degree dependent on, and to some degree independent
of, each other.

The physical body, or *khat*, seems to have been regarded as a thing subject to inevitable corruption, and
yet the greatest pains were taken to preserve it and to
perpetuate its original features. Closely associated
with the *khat*, as a guardian and director, was the *ka*;
a spiritual counterpart of the body, recognisably personal, and having the same aspect as that of the body
to which it belonged. The *ka* survived the death of the
body, at least for a certain period, and paid frequent
visits to the entombed carcase. A figure or image
resembling the deceased, but generally of small dimensions, was made for the reception of the *ka* and placed
with, or near, the body in the tomb. Such images,
made with such intention, were not peculiar to Egypt.
The Kywash of the Cheroune Indians was certainly a
ka-figure ; the Chinese made simulachra of their noblemen, in which the spirit, or a part of it, was supposed
to reside ; in the Kei Islands of Indonesia, every village
has its founder's effigy, wherein his ghost dwells for
ever ; while in modern Africa, many people (the Bongo,
for example) set up images of the dead. Perhaps the
idea is actually present in all the statues of the eminent
or notorious which rise before us (hideous and sinister
obstructions) in the streets of our cities.

As the *ka* resembled the material body in appearance,
so it resembled it in its needs and appetites. If it was
not provided with food, clothes, and unguents, it would
stray away from the tomb, as some-ill-treated domestic
animal strays away from the house, and might become
thin, sick, and miserable. Unlike the homely *ka*, the
sahu was an indestructible, shining double of the body,
essentially a spirit, swift and free. It could travel
where it listed, either on the earth on in the land of the

dead. But the state of the *sahu* was not assured and complete unless it was accompanied by the *khaibit* or shadow. It is not clear, I think, whether this shadow is the one cast by the solid body or whether it is something not perceptible to the eyes of living men. The *ba* is a mysterious entity, less personal than the others : it was connected with the *ka*, and was, indeed, contained within it ; but it had independent and unrestricted movement. The *ba* might perish ; it might enter human bodies : a living man might be host to more than one *ba*.

Like the Kâma of theosophy, the *ab* or heart was the sum of the passions and emotions, though it seems also to have embodied the thinking and reasoning parts of man. The *khu* was the soul of the spirit : imperishable, immortal, etherial, and passionless ; the ultimately surviving form of the soul. Energy or vitality was called *sekhem*.

The *ka*, *ba*, and *khaibit* seem to have constituted a perishable triad, their lives were conditioned by the rites of tendance : that is, they were dependent on the goodness and piety of living men, and if these were remiss in making offerings and in the proper observance of the customs in regard to the dead, *ka*, *ba*, and *khaibit* would come to an end. But the *khu* and the *sahu* were by nature everlasting. They were independent of human care, independent of human needs and passions ; though personal, they represented the incorruptible and divine elements of the personality, and it may be truly said that they returned to the god who made them. They were identified with Osiris.

After death, a certain form or aspect of the personality was connected with the tomb, and there, so it seems, it might be assailed by ghostly monsters. But another aspect of the personality was in the everlasting kingdom of the dead, or travelling, or being judged. The offerings made to the dead were actually presented to the *ka*-figure, though it is clear that they were intended to benefit the whole surviving personality. That the living might themselves acquire merit by such acts of piety is a thought which does not make its appearance in the earliest times ; it may, indeed, indicate a flagging of the original sentiment, and may have been introduced to stimulate a decaying sense of duty.

The other world (Tuat) was conceived of as a land lying beyond the sunset, on the same plane as that of the land of Egypt, and lighted by the same moving sun. It had many divisions and many ruling deities, described and pictured with astonishing wealth of detail and circumstance in the ritual book of Am-Tuat. If we take the account of the other world given in the papyrus of Nu, we find that it consisted of fourteen or fifteen distinct regions. In one of these the spirit was regaled with beer and cakes ; another had walls of iron ; another was occupied only by the gods ; in another lived the great serpent Rerek on a bed of fire ; in another were roaring waters ; another was unknown, even to the gods, and its only inhabitant was " the god who liveth in his egg." The fields of peace were intersected by still waters, and grew abundant crops.

In order that the deceased might not lose his way among the terrors of the shades, and in order that he might know who he was speaking to, and have the proper replies ready on the tip of his tongue, he was provided with an illustrated guide-book : the so-called Book of the Dead. By turning to this book, he found pictures of the gods or demons, so that he could recognise them when he met them, and he then knew how to address them in the proper manner. It was essential that the spirit should know the names of the gates of the other world and those of their warders, and of the hosts of the gods of the shades ; that he should be acquainted with the formulas and with the words of power on which his salvation depended. Every evening, the ghosts, with their credentials and passports, waited at " the Gap " (the entrance to the other world) for the boat of the sun-god Ra. It was convenient to get a passage in this boat, though it was possible to enter the Tuat by other ways. The boat might be left when it had reached the kingdom of Osiris, but there were those who elected to remain in it for ever, sooner than risk judgment. A happy residence in the fields of the blessed could only be ensured by the favourable judgment of Osiris. A soul who was not properly equipped was unable to pass through the divisions of the Tuat : he dwelt in feebleness and in darkness until such time as he was devoured. A like fate befel those who wandered into the other world alone and without guidance.

As the boat of Ra passes through the ghostly regions, lighting each division in turn and leaving it in darkness as the doors close on its wake, it is hailed by the dead with shouts of praise—shouts that give place to a bitter crying as the light passes. The boat is piloted through each region by the divinities of that region : the gods and goddesses of the hours of the night.

In the fifth division is Seker, the grim, ancient god of the dead : his kingdom is bare, sterile, and horrific, full of monsters ; and as the sun-boat passes, a sound as of an echoing storm rises beneath the black vault. Here, there are hells of liquid fire for the damned. In the eighth division are mysterious gods who reply to the speech of Afu-Ra with sounds like the cries of tom-cats, " confused murmur of the living," " sound of those who go down to the battlefield of Nu," " birds in a nest of water-fowl," " sound of the swathed ones," " of those in terror."

The judgment hall of Osiris was in the sixth division, and there the heart of the deceased (the *ab*) was weighed against the feather which was the symbol of righteousness. The weighing and recording were entrusted to the gods Thoth and Anubis, and the first, as recorder, announced the result to the judiciary gods. Judgment was delivered by Osiris at midnight on the souls of those who had died in the course of the preceding day.

The fate of the soul depended on the life of the individual on earth. There is no higher standard of moral and social rectitude than that which was set before the good Egyptian. He was called on, by the judges of the dead, to make a declaration of innocence. By this declaration he proved himself to have been a mild, useful, and faithful member of society, mindful of his obligations, both to his neighbour and to his god. He proclaimed his innocence in regard to no fewer than forty-two separate offences. He was neither a murderer nor an adulterer ; he was not guilty of impure conduct, or of causing fear, or of defrauding. Moreover, he had neither cursed nor uttered falsehood, nor slandered his fellows. He had not been a man of wrath, or heedless of true words, or one who spoke loudly ; and he had not worked for honours and rewards.

There were surveyors in the heavenly fields who measured for each soul his appointed holding. This holding was proportionate, not to the rank, but to the personal merits of the deceased. It seems, however, that rank did make a difference. The pyramid texts of Unas, Teta, and Pepi I show us that the soul of an Egyptian king had immense prestige in the realm of Osiris. It became spiritually related to the great gods and goddesses, living with them on terms of the closest intimacy and sharing their attributes : in fact, it became identified with the names and functions of the chief deities, and entered upon a series of adventures, conflicts, and ceremonies in the course of which it attained almost supreme power.

But the welfare of the dead, even of the kingly dead, was dependent, to some extent, on the observance of prescribed ceremonies by the living, and on the maintenance of a proper supply of offerings. The *simulachrum* of the deceased, the *ka*-figure, received these offerings and was considered as the visible presence of the departed. Derived from the primitive form of " tendance," the offertory rites came to be regarded in time as pious observances which procured no small personal advantage for those who practised them. Those who were diligent in performing all that was required of them as kinsmen of the dead, and who paid attention to the instruction of the priest, might reasonably hope for a reward in the after-life. Moreover, these rites were the means of bringing about an actual communion. Dead and living shared mutually in the funeral feast. Nor was this all, for the gods themselves drew near, attracted by the sweet odour of incense ; and in this delicate enjoyment the living, the dead, and the divine were all partakers at one and the same moment.

As life and power were restored to the dead Osiris through the ministrations of Horus and his four children, who raised him from death to a form of immortal splendour, so life and power and immortality were procured for the dead Egyptian through the ministrations of his friends.

The rituals of " Opening the Mouth " (designed to establish and fortify the spirit in the other world) were observed in Egypt, with no essential change, for more than three thousand years. According to the text of Unas, the rituals which were performed for the soul of a dead king were as follows : First, the *ka*-figure was purified with water, and then with incense, while the royal spirit, accompanied by the greater divinities, approached the ministrants. Then came a further cleansing, with scented water. This water represented the sacred moisture of Horus, and it gave back to the deceased those bodily constituents which had flowed from him during the process of mummification. (In common with many primitive races of modern times, the ancient Egyptians appear to have regarded the liquors which came from a dead body as peculiarly sacred

and precious.) The fourth and fifth rites were libatory,
and identified the soul with the divine essence of the
gods ; and in the sixth rite, a ball of incense was held
before the face of the *ka*-figure. The seventh and eighth
ceremonies were concerned with the opening of the
mouth, and then came one hundred and five ceremonies
in connection with the offerings. The dead king (Unas)
was given butter, water, milk, cakes of all sorts, onions,
beer and wine in different kinds of vessels. He was
annointed with seven unguents. His eyes were painted.
He received linen sashes. He had joints of beef and ribs
of beef, roast meat, liver, spleen, geese, a dove, fruit,
mulberry cakes (immense quantities of cakes, wine,
and beer figure largely in the list of offerings), and finally
" gifts of all sorts." In the text of Pepi II, we read :
" Rejoice and dance, O Pepi Nefer-ka-Ra, for standing
up and sitting down thou hast thousands of vessels of
beer, and joints of meat. . . . As the god is filled with
his divine offerings of bread and cakes and ale, so shall
Pepi Nefer-ka-Ra be filled with his bread." The
substance of the food and drink offerings was translated
into " the essence and substance of Horus . . . both
the spirits of the dead and of the living ate and drank
their god in the form of the spiritual nature of the
material offerings " (Wallis Budge).

The ceremonies of " Opening the Mouth " were carried
out under the supervision of the Kher Heb, a powerful
and dreaded high-priest, who was the mediator between
men and the world of gods and spirits, assisted by the
heir of the deceased, five officiating priests, two groups
of ministrants, and two women who represented Isis and
Nephthys. As a further illustration of these rites in
their most typical form, the following points may be
noted, taken from the observance of the rites for Seti I
(about 1350 B.C.). I have availed myself, as in the previous instance, of the translation and comments of Sir
Wallis Budge.

According to the version found in the tomb of Seti, the first eight ceremonies are purificatory : in the ninth, a priest in the inner tomb seems to personify the dead king. The tenth rite is difficult to understand ; it is known as " smiting of the statue " (i.e. the *ka*-figure), and includes many strange formulas. The " smiting " is in memory of the death of Osiris. In the eleventh rite we have the sacrifice of living creatures : a bull, symbol of Osiris, but also associated with Typhon the evil one, is killed ; the heart of the bull gives warmth and power to the *ka* ; his left fore-leg is eaten as an act of vengeance. Two gazelle and a goose represent the companions of Typhon, and their sacrifice recalls the victory of Horus. The twelfth rite, performed with magical instruments and with gestures, opens the mouth and eyes of the statue and endows the deceased with a new, vigorous, and god-like body. Rites thirteen to sixteen are performed by the heir, assisted by various attendants. In the seventeenth rite we have a curious and very interesting example of a practice which we have already considered, for a priest takes a bag full of some red substance, and with this he rubs the lips and eyelids of the statue. There follow nine other ceremonies, which include the sacrifice of a second bull. Then the statue is dressed with sacred bandlets and with a collar ; then it is anointed ; and then presented with the flail-sceptre, the emblem of dominion, and with the mystic offering of the Mennu. After this, some minor ceremonies take place, and then come one hundred and ten separate offerings. Finally, the statue is taken to the shrine, and is there set in position. There are variants of the ritual, but they all resemble, in sequence and purpose, the form of the above.

Every pious family in Egypt made offerings, at stated times, to the *ka*-figures of their deceased relatives ; thus providing for the welfare of the *ka* and the *ba*, and performing an action which was grateful to the dead,

to the gods of the other world, and to the living members
of the family. And in thus honouring and caring for
the departed, they entered into close communion with
the " king of eternity and governor of the world "—
Osiris.

THE CULT OF OSIRIS

The worship of Osiris certainly represents the most
important and the most consistent element in Egyptian
religion. In this worship, the veneration of ancestors
and the cult of the gods of the dead expanded into their
most beautiful and most impressive forms. Osiris
was the chief of the Egyptian divinities for at least
four thousand years ; his cult persisted through periods
of heresy or innovation, and faded only when the
teaching of a new Redeemer had reached the valley of
the Nile. As late as the sixth century of our own era,
a form of the worship of Osiris and Isis, and of the dead
(with whom they were always associated), was still in
existence in the neighbourhood of Thebes.

Osiris was the god beloved of the people. He gave
them hope and comfort ; promising reward to the righteous, peace to weary and troubled men, justice to the
oppressed, and happy reunion to the bereaved. His
worshippers were never wholly seduced by the flam-
boyant lordship of Ra, the hot splendours of Aten.
Indeed, we learn from the Greenfield Papyrus that Osiris
and Amen-Ra were looked on as united in one mystic
godhead—the creative power of Amen continued by
the resurrective power of Osiris. There was a time when
Osiris was connected, in the popular mind, with the
moon ; and a time when he lived among the stars of
Orion : but always he was the lord and ruler of the
dead. His kingdom, to the early Egyptian, was a place
of horrors and darkness, of misery and decay. But with
the ascendency and full expansion of his godhead,
Osiris became the just and good governor ; the fields of

the righteous dead were bright, the shades of blameless men were industrious and happy. The soul of the dead man became united to the god ; so that the ghost of Ani the Scribe could say, " I have knit myself together ; I am whole ; my youth is renewed within me ; I am Osiris the everlasting."

From the ancient Delta city of Busiris the worship of the immortal ancestors, and of their lord, friend and redeemer, spread throughout the whole land of Egypt. " Hail to thee ! " cried the soul in the hall of judgment, " thou who art uplifted in the high place, who art named Ruler of the Winds ; save me from thy assessors, they whose faces are uncovered, who charge me with evil and lay bare my secret faults, for I have done the Truth." And Thoth made question, " Who is he whose covering is fire, whose walls are serpents, whose floor is rushing water ? Who is he ? " And the soul answered " Osiris."

The judgment of Ra took place at sunrise, and that of Osiris at midnight. Then the righteous were made happy and the wicked were doomed—not to suffering, but to instant annihilation.

The worship of Osiris was already ancient at the time of the Fourth Dynasty ; the time of its full elaboration. The cult most probably dates back to an age prior to that of written records. Its extent and dominance in ancient times are well attested in Mariette's description of the great cemetery of Saqqarah, which I here translate : " The necropolis of Saqqarah must have been formerly, like all the necropoles of Egypt, a veritable city of the dead. A dozen pyramids rose in the midst of it, attracting the notice of the distant traveller. It had streets bordered by monumental tombs ; it had quarters, cross-roads, and squares. . . . The necropolis had also its functionaries and servants, charged with the care of the tombs, with their proper maintenance, with the allocation of plots to families, and also with ceremonies in connection with funerals and with the cult of the dead." Another French Egyptologist, Amélineau, describes the cemetery of Memphis as " la plus vaste du monde," and says that it extended over a space of not less than 50 to 60 kilometres. This area, which includes the pyramids of Gizeh, contains tombs of all sorts and of all periods, from the Fourth to the Twenty-sixth Dynasty. Here, also, is the Serapeum, where the mummies of the holy Apis bulls are encased in huge granite sarcophagi.

Thus it will be seen that the cult of the great ancestor-god, Osiris, himself the life of the souls of the departed and himself the resurrection, became the vital and dominant principle in Egyptian religion. This noble religion—for it was certainly noble—grew out of the primitive fear of the dead. First of all, as we have seen, Osiris was a king of terrors ; the lord of a dark and hideous domain. Under the influence of civilisation he became the just god, meting out happiness for the good and destruction for the evil. The worship of Osiris, derived from and inseparably connected with the cult of the dead, endured in full vigour for an immense period : a period far longer than that covered by any existing form of religion.

Osiris had suffered at the hands of wicked men and had been treacherously killed ; he had risen from the dead, and promised a sure resurrection to his worshippers. His justice as a god was assured by the knowledge of human suffering he had acquired during his life as a sinless man. He was surrounded by forms and expressions of divinity which display, in their fullest development, all the symbolic and representational elements of religion. The idea of sacramental communion has never existed in a more beautiful or more dignified form than that in which it existed as part of the Osirian rituals. No divine mother and child have received a purer devotion than that which was offered to Isis and her son Horus. No faith has been illuminated by a more sublime, a more truly poetic imagery. I believe that we have, in the cult of Osiris, a religion which is not only the most typical in point of evolution, but the most religious of all religions—resting as it does upon the primal religious instinct of mankind : the ancient fear of the dead.

The sequence of burial customs in Egypt is of remarkable interest. It represents the unchecked development, among a people changing but little in breed or in essential character, of funerary practice and of religious thought. It extends from the neolithic age to the beginning of the Christian period. We have seen something of the attitude of the Egyptian towards the souls of the dead and towards the gods of the other world, and we shall be able to appreciate, in some degree, the motives which controlled the detail and arrangement of Egyptian burials.

PREDYNASTIC AND DYNASTIC BURIALS IN EGYPT

" The Egyptians were afraid of fire, not as a deity' but as a devouring element, mercilessly consuming their bodies, and leaving too little of them ; and therefore by precious embalments, depositure in dry earths, or handsome inclosure in glasses, contrived the notablest ways of integral conservation." Thus wrote Sir Thomas Browne in his famous essay on *Urn Burial*. The cult of Osiris laid stress on the importance of " integral conservation." Osiris himself was restored to life in his material body, after the scattered remains of that body had been brought together again. In some way, the health and composure of the soul depended on the care of the dead body, and on its protection, as far as possible, from the forces of corruption. The well-being of the *ka* and the *ba* depended absolutely, as we have

seen, on the preservation and the spiritual nourishment
of the body, with which they remained closely associated
after death.   But the state of the entombed body
affected all the elements of the surviving personality,
and it thus became the immediate concern of the living.

This aspect of cultus is based, no doubt, on what I
must term the anthropomorphic instinct—the feeling
that the human form, whether dead or alive, or anything
which represents or resembles it, any image or picture,
centralises a part of the human spirit.   Such a feeling
was certainly experienced in regard to the *ka*-statue ;
and very much more so in regard to the dead body.
It is a feeling which is experienced, in a greater or lesser
degree, by every one of us.   The destruction of the body
by fire is regarded as irreligious and prejudicial by the
majority of Christians.

We have seen, however, that primitive men are by
no means unanimous on this point.   In a great number
of cases, the destruction, not the preservation, of the body
is a pious duty.   Until the carcase has been consumed,
or has decayed, the spirit is still the slave of the flesh.
Until nothing is left but a parcel of dry bones, or a hand-
ful of ashes, the soul is not freed from earthly restraint.
It would seem that this view is less primitive than the
other.   The preservation of the corpse is the primary
instinct.

In this matter, the Egyptians perpetuated the older
and more primitive tradition.   Even in prehistoric
times an effort was made to preserve the body by
the application of some bituminous substance.   The
carcase of a neolithic Egyptian, preserved by this means,
lies inside a glass case in the British Museum.   At the
same time, from the evidence of certain predynastic
burials, it would seem that the bodies were sometimes
dismembered and decapitated.   The skull is occasionally
found in a place by itself ; the skeleton is disarticulated
and broken.   To some investigators it has appeared

evident that the flesh must have been scraped from the
bones before the latter were buried. But others maintain
that these appearances are often illusory : the graves
have been disturbed by maurauders, by prowling beasts,
by movements of sand or soil.

The earliest Egyptian grave is merely a shallow pit,
scooped out of the ground, and in this the corpse was
placed on its side, in the orthodox contracted position.
Before burial, the body was usually wrapped in a mat
made of grass or reeds. The furniture of these simple
interments consisted of pottery vessels and flint knives,
blades, or flakes. Children (there might be two or three
together) were buried in separate graves. In the larger
graves, there are found occasionally double interments,
the bodies, with the limbs always more or less bent up,
being placed side by side.

Even these early graves, so poorly furnished in com-
parison with those of the full dynastic civilisation, have
been plundered by people who make it their business
to sell trifles to trippers. Indeed, what with the activities
of the professional looter and the unceasing attentions of
folk whose credentials are only slightly more respectable,
it is becoming no easy matter to find an inviolate
Egyptian grave. During the past few years, tombs have
been opened and rifled, less with any scientific gain in
view than for the benefit of the popular press and the
popular publisher. An extremely vulgar and tactless
procedure has led to equally vulgar squabbles. Discoveries of no extraordinary significance have been
described in our cheaper periodicals and papers with
a wealth of exaggeration, inaccuracy, and shabby
journalese. It will not be long, I suppose, before archæological research in Egypt is conducted by limited
liability companies, organised by gentlemen who are
interested in colour-photography, in the cinema, and
in the sale of fortnightly educators.

I have digressed in order to draw attention to a state

of affairs which constitutes a real menace to serious research in Egypt. It is not exactly a new menace. Amélineau spoke of it many years ago, deploring the inactivity both of the museum authorities at Cairo and of the Egyptian Government. The pillaging of tombs continues unchecked, and much valuable information is lost.

Following the simple prehistoric pit-burial comes a somewhat deeper grave, more or less oblong, with rounded corners, or oval. The disposition of the body, or bodies, is unaltered. Next we have a square grave, sometimes lined with bricks or wood, and occasionally with a covering of wooden laths, layers of reeds or grass and of mud. Then comes a most important and characteristic modification : the grave is again deepened, so that the body lies at the foot of a vertical shaft, and immediately over the shaft is a place for the recital of prayers and the presentation of offerings. This is the beginning of the *mastaba* type.

Before going on to the consideration of the *mastaba* we will examine the contents of some of the predynastic graves excavated at El Mahasna by Ayrton and Loat. In keeping with the general facts of prehistoric burial, we find that the neolithic people of Egypt buried their children with care. One of these predynastic graves held the body of a child which " had been laid on a tray of matting stiffened with strips of wood round the sides." Pottery vases were found with the skeletons of children in the shallow round graves of the early period ; and in one of these burials the bodies of three children, wrapped in a large mat, were accompanied by vases, beads of cornelian and of black stone, a stone palette, a small basket, a crystal pendant, and large discs of shell. Two pottery coffins of this date were found ; one of them evidently intended for the body of a child. Some of the graves were lined with planks of wood, enclosing the body and a few vases, while the

larger vessels were placed outside. Graves were also
lined with reeds and mud, or with bricks. In an oval
grave, which had unfortunately been plundered, they
found the bones of a woman and of a child mixed up
together : there were also five small pottery bowls and
a small red polished bowl with a white criss-cross pattern,
a large vessel with grain inside it, slate palettes, a slate
pendant, broken ivory bracelets, a fragment of an
ivory comb, a cornelian pendant, two beads of gold
and three of cornelian, and a glazed composition bead.
This, in view of the fact that it had been rifled, must
have been a comparatively richly furnished burial.

But they had the good fortune to find a large square
grave which had not been previously disturbed. In
this lay a skeleton, presumably female, with the legs
slightly drawn up, and the arms stretched out, the
hands being in line with the face : in front of this skeleton
was another in the same position. Between the fore-
arms of the first skeleton was a mass of crushed ivory
bracelets ; on the ribs was a clay mace-head, and behind
the shoulders were two large bits of clay painted red.
At the top of the head were several more bracelets ;
at the back of it, strings of cornelian and green glazed
steatite beads. At a little distance from the head was
the ivory figurine of an elongated man (apparently
ithyphallic), and four so-called wands of ivory with
eyelets at one end. Behind the body was a rhomboid
slate palette. The other skeleton had a black-topped
vase by its head, two polished red vases, and a very
beautiful bowl of polished red pottery with four cleverly
modelled figures of hippo on the rim : beyond these
objects were ox bones under a mat. At the feet of the
body were two shells containing bits of green malachite
and some beads, and two polished pebbles—these latter
may have been used for grinding the malachite (which
was meant for painting the eyelids). Beyond these
things was a bowl, a limestone vase, two ivory combs

and two ivory hair-pins, and two small vases of the same material ; there was also the ivory figure of a donkey, and there were several beads of resin and hæmatite. In the side of the grave was a white lime-stone vase ; and against one end of it were three large black-topped vases, under which were great pieces of resin and sulphate of lime, and " a great deal of burnt organic matter," together with a very big slate palette of the usual rhomboid shape, two valves of mussel shells, and a small bowl. One grave contained a headless skeleton, but, as this grave had been plundered, it cannot be asserted that the body was headless when it was buried. I think it is probable that the heads or skulls were, in many cases, taken by plunderers.

In some of these burials little clay images were found : images which display that peculiar anatomical exuber-ance which is known as steatopygy ; a characteristic of Hottentot women at the present day. The bones of oxen, goats, and antelopes were associated with some of the burials. So also were flint implements, but these did not occur frequently : some of them were finely worked.

The *mastaba*, which dates from the time of the first dynasties (roughly 4000 B.C.) is the characteristic Egyptian tomb. In principle it does not vary : at the bottom of a deep shaft or at the end of a sloping corridor is the burial ; above this shaft or passage is an edifice which serves the purpose of a shrine or chapel, dedicated to the deceased. Thus the *mastaba* is partly above and partly below the surface of the ground. The exterior edifice may be regarded as the earliest construction of a purely religious character—the prototype of the fully developed shrine or temple. It may be that all religious institutions are derived from the form and circumstance of primitive burial.

Many primitive races have evolved the idea of a spirit-house above the grave, and a type of burial closely resembling the *mastaba* is found in modern Africa. Schweinfurth describes the grave-construction of the Bongo people : he says that a short shaft was dug, and a recess hollowed out at the end of it for the reception of the body ; after the shaft was filled in, a pile of stones was raised over it, and in the middle of this pile they set a pitcher, often the one from which the deceased was accustomed to drink. The same writer tells us that the Niam-Niam buried in a shaft and recess grave, and that they built a hut above the shaft. Ghost-houses over the grave are still found in the Uganda Protectorate and elsewhere in Africa.

In the course of their development, the surface buildings became more and more elaborate, and assumed greater proportions, culminating in the colossal forms of the pyramids. Within the pyramid is the mortuary shrine or chapel, and beneath it, approached by a long descending corridor, is the subterranean tomb. The passage leading to the tomb of Neterkhet, of the Third Dynasty, descended for about a hundred feet below the surface, while the superstructure was thirty feet above ground level. Sometimes the exterior building is represented by a rock-hewn chamber, beneath which a shaft or well descends to the place of burial. Where the tombs are congregated together within the enclosure of a great cemetery, as at Saqqarah, the shrines opened on to the street or path, so that the passers-by had free access to them. After the body had been placed at the foot of the shaft, pit, or well, the shaft (whether vertical or inclined) was filled up with blocks of stone, or any sort of compact rubbish ; and the grave itself, if recessed at the foot of the shaft, was blocked by a great boulder or a mass of heavy stones. Thus the place of burial was made inaccessible. But there were also common tombs in these cemeteries, where bodies were piled up in hundreds, and the entrances to these tombs have always been open. In the *mastaba*, the burial-chamber was regarded as a place secure from all disturbance : " Le mort y reposait dans une obscurité éternelle " (Mariette).

The upper structure of the *mastaba*, in its early, but complete, form, consists of a masonry building of rectangular plan, the sides inclining inwards, and usually built up outside in a series of steps. The greater axis, without exception, is north-south. Particular care was bestowed on the exterior facing ; but on the inner walls the work was often extremely slip-shod. The east face was the most important. Near the north-east angle there is usually a tall quadrangular niche ; and near the south-east angle is, either another niche with an inscribed monolithic stele (or tomb-stone), or a façade with a door : in the latter case there is no inner chamber, this recess taking the place of it. Nothing is ever found on the west side. The top of the building is flat ; the earth thereon is found to contain vases, thinly distributed, and apparently filled with water when placed there. (I am reminded, no doubt irrelevantly, of the " pixy pots " on the roofs of Cornish hovels). There may be one or several chambers inside. A table or altar for offerings stands in the chapel. Pictures and inscriptions are found at the entrance, on the stele, and on the walls. On either side of the entrance the dead man is represented standing, and with him are his names and titles. On the architrave is the prayer for offerings " at the beginning of the year, at the festival of Thoth on the first day of the year, at the festival of navigation, at the great panegyric, at the festival of heat, at the appearing of the god Khem, at the festival of the holocaust, the festivals of the months and half-months, and all the festival days." The stele is usually on the east wall. Brilliant in colour and with vivacious detail, the pictures and reliefs on the walls gave an effect of cheerfulness, even of gaiety. At this time (the period of the Ancient Empire), the life of the defunct was thought of as a peaceful and idealised continuance of his earthly life ; the gods of the underworld had not yet become exacting and troublesome. " Pour les parents assemblés dans les chambres interieures des mastabas, le mort revit. Ils le revoient assis aux mêmes tables, entourés des même serviteurs, naviguant sur les mêmes eaux, prenant part aux mêmes chasses " (Mariette).

The *ka*-figure was housed in the *serdab* ; a square recess of massive construction built in the wall, with low roof and straight sides, sometimes without communication of any sort with the other parts of the *mastaba* or with the outside, though generally having a small conduit (hardly wide enough for the insertion of one's arm) which leads to the chamber of offerings. Oddly enough, figures have been found in these recesses with names not corresponding to those of the buried body. The smell of the offerings and of the burning incense reached the invisible *ka*-figure in the *serdab*, and the soul was thus cheered and refreshed.

There is no connection between the chamber of offerings and the burial-chamber. The latter (40 or 50 feet below the surface) has to be approached by working down through the outer platform—the roof of the superstructure. Having descended the vertical shaft, after the removal of the stones and rubbish with which it is blocked, one crawls along a level gallery, at the end of which is the tomb itself, where a man can stand upright. This tomb, though it is entirely unconnected with it, is always immediately beneath the exterior chamber. In relation to the ground-plan of the *mastaba* the tomb is small. The stone sarcophagus, containing the body, is placed in one corner. On the floor there are sometimes a few pottery vessels, and perhaps the bones of an ox. Within the sarcophagus there may be a head-rest and a few small objects of alabaster.

Garstang, excavating tombs of the Third Dynasty (3400 B.C.) at Reqaqnah, found burial places with stairways leading to the underground chambers. This form of sepulchre is derived from a predynastic type, with two or three steps. Actual stairway tombs make their appearance in the First Dynasty. The steps led down to the grave under a series of rough arches. In the rectangular enclosures, the bodies were generally laid out straight, or slightly flexed at the legs, obviously (in this case) with the idea of making them fit the space. In the vaulted chambers, the bodies were also extended ; the head was invariably to the north, facing east.

But the most peculiar discoveries at Reqaqnah were those of burials underneath large earthenware pots. "From the latter end of the predynastic period, continuing through the First, Second, and Third Dynasties, so far as those can be distinguished, the crude method of interment in a large inverted bowl seems to have survived. . . . The custom was never general : the recorded instances are few. . . . Whether, indeed, it was reserved for some special class or caste cannot be asserted upon present evidence " (Garstang). The bones were found lying on the ground beneath the pot in a huddled pile. Was the body forced into the vessel, and the latter then turned upside-down ; or was the pot placed over the prepared remains as they lay on the ground ? Garstang thinks that the body was squeezed into the pot, which was then overturned. But Randall MacIver, speaking of burials of this class at El Amrah, said that " whenever these burials have not been disturbed, the pot is always inverted over the body, which is laid in a violently contracted position."

At Nuerat, rock-hewn tombs of the Third and Fourth Dynasties have been discovered. In these, the shaft or well is shallow, and in some instances it is placed immediately below the entrance to the tomb. At the bottom of each undisturbed shaft there was a large pottery receptacle with a lid, enclosing a body in the contracted position. In front of these tombs were a number of the pot-burials which we have just examined.

Painted wooden coffins (long, massive, rectangular chests) were used in the early dynasties. Fine examples of these have been found in Fifth Dynasty burials near Beni Hassan and the Speos Artemidos. In one of these burials, a wooden *ka*-figure stood in position near the coffin : at the end of the chamber were some pottery jars, sealed with mud, which had contained drink of some sort ; there were also dishes for food. The only decoration on the coffin consisted of the two " sacred eyes " (of Horus) and the body lay on its side, showing no trace of mummification.

During the Eleventh and Twelfth Dynasties (roughly 2600 to 2400 B.C.) the chamber at the bottom of the shaft was sometimes enlarged for additional burials ; or these might be placed at higher levels, connected with the shaft. About this time, the undertaker, who was often a dishonest and sacrilegious rascal, makes his appearance. The tomb-robber also comes on the scene. Between the dishonest undertaker and the robber there seems to have been an occasional alliance ; for the former so constructed his coffins that the latter might be able to get his hand inside them. Or it is possible that the undertaker's men were the robbers, filching the jewels and other precious things after they had placed the coffin in the grave. Nor was this the only form of dishonesty connected with funeral affairs. The embalmers, charged with the removal of the visceral contents and their deposit in wrappings or in the " canopic jars," often neglected to carry out their duties, and the jars or wrappings were empty when placed in the tomb. Already scepticism had arisen, and there were men who, through greed or indolence, defied the anger of the ghost.

The less illustrious people of the Middle Empire were buried in pit-graves in close proximity to each other ; so close that the surface of the ground was honeycombed with their openings. It would seem that these cemeteries were laid out by speculators, for it is no uncommon thing to find, especially at the ends of rows, that the chambers have been left unfinished. Garstang is convinced that there was " a definite industry, the chief business of which was to furnish and equip the chambers of the dead." For some hundreds of years, the coffins, tombs, and votive offerings were more or less standardised, and they were evidently made on a system of mass production. When the coffin was decorated with its hieroglyphs (prayers for offerings, or addresses to the gods), a space was left blank for the name of the deceased. The manufacture of coffins was therefore a definite trade. The name was frequently "hastily written in ink in a careless hand," and sometimes it was not written at all, and the space was left blank. The undertaker's men, when they were engaged in making shafts close to previous ones, which had already received their burials, made a habit of burglariously picking their way through the partition separating the new shaft from the old one, and plundering the grave. One of Professor Petrie's workers told me that he found the body of a thief in a Twelfth Dynasty grave : the man had been crushed and killed by a fall of rock ; he lay across the coffin which he had prised open ; his fingers were still clenched round a number of jewels, and he had secreted others in various parts of his clothing. The practice of robbing tombs became so prevalent that it was punishable by death under the rulers of the New Empire.

As a typical example of a Middle Empire burial I will take that of Antef, a courtier. The shaft leading to his grave was filled so compactly, and with such weighty stones, that the burglars had not been able to work their way down. At the foot of the shaft a small chamber opened, as ususal, to the south. Within this was a wooden coffin, with wooden models laid upon it or standing by the side. A model of a granary was placed obliquely on the top of the sarcophagus : in the same place was a pair of sandals, a model of an eight-oar rowing boat with crew and steersman, a group of women making bread, and a man leading a bull. By the side of the coffin there was a model of a sailing boat with a crew of six and a timoneer ; there were also models of a man brewing, and of a market woman with a brace of birds in one hand and a basket on the top of her head. The granary was a complete model ; inside it there were three figures—two labourers and a clerk, the latter seated on the roof of the store-house with his ink-board and writing-block on his lap. These figures, and those of a like kind, including the *ushabtiu* figures, so often found in Egyptian burials, were intended to represent people who would work for the deceased in the fields of the blessed, and pay attention to his needs. Flint implements were not, as a rule, buried at this period ; they were retained for sacrifice and other ritual purposes.

Let us examine a typical female burial of the same date ; that of Senb, a Lady of the Household. Jewels had been placed on the body, and Senb was provided with such things as were necessary for her toilet. She had three little boxes of wood, inlaid with ivory and ebony, and of dainty workmanship. She had also some ivory hairpins, and a palette and crusher for preparing antimony, wherewith she would darken her eyebrows and lashes. Cosmetic boxes were found in many tombs ; one of them consisted of four united cylinders, covered by a single lid moving on a pivot.

The sacred eyes of Horus were almost invariably painted on the outside of the coffin, and the head of the body lying within was turned towards them. Usually the coffins lay on a north-south alignment, and the face of the corpse was turned towards the east. The great gods to whom the funeral inscriptions are addressed are Anubis and Osiris.

The actual funeral rites are depicted on the walls of

certain tombs. Sculptured on the rock of the tomb of
Mentuherkhepeshef, a Theban dignitary, is an extraordinarily interesting representation of a funeral procession :

Three men walk at the head of the cortège, evidently
mourners of importance. Following them are three
other men, hauling along a kind of sled, whereon is
the crouching figure of a man. This man appears in
all the burial processions of notable folk, but he is usually
muffled from head to foot in a black wrapper. In this
particular scene he does not seem to be restrained in any
way. The sled is followed by four men who are dragging
a large panelled chest (or *naos*) on runners : they are
accompanied by a " lector." Then comes a mysterious
group of seven men, whose ceremonial function is unknown. Next, we have an incident of ritual : five
officiants make offerings to a ram which is penned up
in an enclosure. Now, the sarcophagus comes on the
scene, drawn by three pairs of oxen and attended by
nine men—three men behind each pair of oxen holding
the ropes. The coffin is carried in a large decorated
chest, set upon runners. A man who hits two sticks
together (perhaps for the purpose of signalling directions,
or to make music) is called " the instructor." The
" embalmer " and the " royal acquaintance " (the
king's representative ?) are also in the procession, and
so is a woman described as the " wife of the god." Two
women who precede and follow the bier impersonate the
sisters of Osiris.

We now come to the most interesting portion of the
rock sculpture, which shows the burial rites. First, the
catafalque is carried on the shoulders of the attendants
and placed on a sled, beneath which is a bow. Then we
are shown seven ministrants kneeling before a catafalque
which is dedicated to Anubis. Next comes the ceremony
of breaking the bow and the *ped aha* (a mystic staff or
weapon) in front of a catafalque dedicated to Osiris.

This breaking is done in order that the objects may go with the dead man. After this we have the " opening of the ground," with sacrifice, and the rite of " the great god filling the ground four times "—an action performed by a man with a bowl or basket, out of which he pours something into the trench, while the ghost watches him with keen attention. Then comes the crouching man on the sled (he is called *tekenu*) : the four men who are dragging him along cry " Lo ! the *tekenu* sets forth ! " Bulls are then sacrificed ; and later comes an episode which " has all the appearance of being a scene of torture or execution " (N. de G. Davies). While this is going on, two men kneel with ropes uncomfortably twisted round their throats : either they are going to be strangled by the attendants who hold the ends of the ropes, or they are enacting some pantomime of submission ; and, as they look like Nubian captives, it may well be that the latter is the case. Close to the two kneeling men, two other Nubians, swathed like mummies, are laid out on the ground : in another version of the ceremony, these two prostrate captives are described as paying homage, so " we need not consider these either as necessarily doomed men." Perhaps we may see in these practices the survival of some earlier sacrificial rite. Obscure rituals follow, in which both men and women take part. We then see a pit inscribed with the word *tekenu*, and containing the hair, heart, hide, and foreleg of some animal—perhaps a sacrifice which has taken the place of the human *tekenu*. Now the dead man is provided with salve, incense, cloth, natron, bread, and drink. The " uplifting of the olive tree " follows, and this seems to be a piece of light buffoonery, in which mimes and equilibrists take part : similar diversions or comic interludes are recorded elsewhere. More serious rites then take place at a large pit which seems to be full of fire. An ox is cut up ; and the rites conclude with sacrificing and the presentation of offerings, the throwing of a bull's entrails in the " pit of burning," and other ceremonies of a sacrificial nature.

In another Theban tomb, that of Tati, there is the representation of a very interesting scene—probably a unique representation. We are here shown the actual digging of a burial shaft. I will quote the explanatory note of N. de G. Davies. " On the ground a white mass of rock is seen. On this two brick pillars have been erected . . . and across these a beam has been laid. The head and shoulders of a man, ' Anhu,' appear, emerging from the centre of the rock. The excavated material is lifted out in a bag, which is pulled to the surface by a rope passing over the beam and hauled by the man below. The rope passes over a tapering block cut in or fastened on the beam. . . . A man steadies and receives the bag when it reaches the top and hands it to another, who carried off the contents to the tip-heap. . . . It looks as if this scene had been put in at the request of the quarriers, who desired to be immortalised in this way."

The grandest, most beautiful, and most impressive forms of sepulture were evolved in Egypt under the later dynasties (1600 to 500 B.C.). Noble architecture, of massive and just proportion, was combined with grace and richness of interior ornament. No monument of our own times approaches the sepulchral dignity of the Egyptian tomb.

The Egyptian practice of mummifying the dead body was of great antiquity. In the period of the later dynasties, the mummy was enclosed in a brilliantly decorated cartonnage case, moulded to the shape of the swathed body. Cartonnage consists of many layers of fine linen, tightly compressed and held together by an adhesive, and covered by a thin wash of stucco.

Herodotus says that the process of mummification was carried out by the members of a legally instituted

guild ; men who held proper credentials and qualifica-
tions. There were three methods. In the first and most
expensive, the brain was extracted through the nose,
and the internal parts were drawn out through an in-
cision made with a stone instrument in the side of the
body. After being washed and scented, the visceral
organs were placed in "canopic jars." The body was
then stuffed with sweet-smelling herbs, and, after having
been laid in natron (native sesquicarbonate of soda) for
seventy days, it was washed, and then tightly swathed
in long strips of linen. This procedure, according to Sir
Wallis Budge, cost the equivalent of something like
£240. There was a cheaper method, costing about £90,
in which case the brain was not removed, the intestines
were dissolved, and the body was left in salt and natron
until nothing remained of it except the skin and the
bones. In the case of those who were unable to pay for
the more expensive processes, a powerful astringent
was injected into the body, which was then pickled in
salt for seventy days.

We have only been able to deal very briefly with the
Egyptian cult of the dead, a cult in which the presiding
influence is that of the god-man Osiris. Towards this
great divinity and towards the gods who attended him,
the friends, rulers, and judges of the dead, the Egyptians
directed equally their prayers and their hopes. Osiris
had once been a man, and as a man he had been acquainted with human weakness and error. He was therefore a merciful and discerning god. His dominion was
not confined to the realm of the dead, though he was
the resident king of that realm ; he was the lord of all
souls, embodied or disembodied ; he contained within
himself all the ancient powers of the ancestral dead,
and was thus intimately concerned with the living.
When the Egyptian buried his deceased relatives, he
buried them in the sure hope of the glorious resurrection

which had been promised by Osiris. All the forms of burial which we have described were carried out with that hope in view. To the dominance of the cult of the dead in Egypt we owe those colossal monuments, the pyramids : monuments of such vast proportion that they must be reckoned still among the most wonderful achievements of mankind. We owe to this cult, moreover, the greater part of our knowledge of ancient Egyptian life, for the records of that life are most abundantly preserved in the sepulchres and in the commemorative writings. The Egyptian lived in close, in continual touch with his departed kinsmen, and with the gods into whose kingdom they had passed. In this communion he found the full expression of his religious impulse ; he found, indeed, his religion. With joyous hope and with fervour, yet with profound awe, the soul of the dead man cried to his god :

" Glory be to thee, O Osiris Un-Nefer, thou great god in Abtu, King of Eternity, Lord of Everlastingness, God who livest for millions of years, first son of Nut, begotten by Geb, the Chief of Ancestors, Lord of the Crowns of the South and of the North, Lord of the High White Crown. . . . Homage to thee, King of Kings, who, coming from the womb of the Sky-Mother, hast ruled the Earth and the Otherworld. Thy limbs are as gold and silver, the blueness of thy hand is like unto the blueness of lapis-lazuli. . . . Praise be to thee, Immortal Governor and Prince of Princes."

CHAPTER VI

SACRED MEMORY

The modern attitude towards the problem of survival—
Eschatology of the churches—Psychic research—Ghosts—
Funerals, monuments, and epitaphs.

THE MODERN ATTITUDE TOWARDS THE
PROBLEM OF SURVIVAL

THERE were few subjects which Dr. Johnson was unwilling to discuss, but there was one which he treated always with a kind of solemn petulance : the subject of death and the after-life. This reticence was not peculiar to Johnson ; it was characteristic of the age in which he lived—an age of unruffled elegance and of demure yet steadfast orthodoxy. In that age, a man who considered that the nature of the soul (let alone the question of its existence) was a proper theme for discussion was branded as an infidel ; and to be marked as an infidel in the eighteenth century was to be distinguished in a way that was far from pleasant. But all this has changed. The charge of religious infidelity falls on our modern heads, when it does fall, with a feathery lightness. Not that we are irreligious : in the mass we are neither religious nor infidel—we are indifferent. It is indifference, not hostility, which seems likely to bring about the dissolution (not the violent destruction) of our present systems of religion. The typical believing Christian of the present day is the converted negro. Very few of us, even the most respectable, if we were pinned down to an honest definition of our faith, could say what it was that

we really believed in, or what it was that we really denied.
We rather hope, perhaps, that we are immortal.   We
do not wish to believe that all our fine fancies are snuffed
out by death.   We are disturbed vaguely by the thought
of annihilation ;   but we are also disturbed by the
thought of the embarrassing or uncomfortable eternity
promised by the churches.   Finally, we dismiss the problem, knowing that matters will take their inevitable
course.

Our present civilisation, let it be admitted frankly,
is incompatible with a general belief in the immortality
of the human soul ; at any rate with a general conviction
on that point.   A general conviction is only found among
uncivilised people, and it is accompanied, as often as
not, by theories and practices which strike us as absurd
and revolting.   We know that primitive man is entirely
wrong on many subjects of cardinal importance.   His
cosmogony is all wrong ; his physics are all wrong ;
his astronomy is all wrong ; his mathematics are all
wrong : indeed, his views on these subjects are not
merely wrong, but wildly incorrect.   Is he right or
wrong in his views concerning the immortality of the
soul ?   Or, to bring it down to the essential question, is
he right in believing implicitly, as he does, that the personal being, in some form or another, survives bodily
death ?   We have shown that it is quite possible for
him to be mistaken on this point also ; but, on the
other hand, it is possible that he is not mistaken.   Be
that as it may, the complexity of modern life has driven
this primitive conviction out of our minds.   And yet
most of us would be glad to find a loophole for the
admission of belief ; and even if we do not perceive
such a loophole, that is no proof that it does not exist
somewhere.

In the mind of the most uncouth savage, of the most
ancient or the most primitive man, there existed and
there still exists an unquestioning belief in immortality.

In a critical modern age, clamouring (somewhat un-intelligently) for proof and demonstration, no such belief is held implicitly : it becomes a theme for vulgar debate and familiar discussion in the penny press ; and only persons who are suspected of being unduly religious or unduly credulous assert their faith in the life eternal. We are not primarily concerned here with the contro-versial aspects of this great question, though it is difficult to avoid a tendency to form certain conclusions, or at least to hazard certain guesses. But our aim is rather the collection of suggestive material than the application of test or theory. Disbelief in the personal survival of death is a characteristic of modern, one might almost say of recent thought ; for immeasurable ages men have believed that the personality does survive. Not only are we without proof of a stage of primitive or ancient culture in which this belief is not present, but we are without proof of a really primitive state of incredulity. In what way, then, are we to account for the attitude of the civilised European of to-day ?

Let it be recognised, that the attitude, even of those who imagine themselves to be purged of all superstition, is far from consistent. The cult of the ancestor is yet with us. The ghost, although he is of no account in the light of day, can still become a terror by night, he can still awaken the ancient fears of man. Nor is this all. It is a transmuted though recognisable form of cult which inclines us towards a reverence for anything which is old, less on account of its worth than on account of its antiquity. For this reason, incredibly dull works are reprinted and sold perpetually ; incredibly dull music is obstinately performed and obstinately yet reverently heard ; incredibly ugly pictures, ugly furni-ture, and ugly buildings are unceasingly praised—less because of their supposed beauty than because of their known age. For this reason, the pitifully crude scrawl-ing and chipping of prehistoric man become the most

marvellous of marvels : all through a desire to show
respect to the antique and the dead. The worship of
the past is the worship of ancestors ; and the archæologist is really the most religious of men.

But our heritage of primitive thought (if it is nothing
more) shows itself in other and less obscure ways. Our
attitude towards a dead body very nearly resembles that
of the savage. Most of us are greatly disturbed by the
sight, or even the mere proximity, of a human cadaver.
Skulls are commonly regarded with feelings of horror
and repulsion. We retain also the idea that the personality of any one who is dead clings to his belongings
and lurks in the places he was accustomed to frequent ;
and this applies not only to property in general but to
property in particular. Many people are averse to
handling, and still more to wearing, clothes or trinkets
which were worn or carried by the deceased. It is usual
enough, too, to find that rooms with which the dead
person was closely associated are preserved as far as
possible from disturbance ; at any rate during the years
immediately following the death. The modern attitude
towards ghosts will be discussed later.

In many ways our responses to the aspect or suggestion
of death, our natural reactions, are exactly similar to
those of the savage ; with this essential difference, that,
whereas in his case these reactions are due to a conscious
attitude and are regarded as perfectly explicable (just
as the reaction to a splash of cold water is explicable—
the nature of cause and effect being clearly perceived),
in our case they are looked on as purely superstitious,
or as the indefinable shrinking from the " uncanny."
In short, our responses are partly automatic. Our
minds, we say, are clouded temporarily by the stirring
up of the primitive residue which, normally, lies in a
quiet and sedimentary state at the bottom of the unconscious. It is but a momentary recoil, we say ; and
our reason, dislodged for that moment from the higher

centres of the mind, swings back to her established place and proves our folly.

Such arguments, however, are only conclusive if we are prepared to admit that there is no such thing as a discarnate personality ; that those who are dead are mentally extinct ; that we cannot, in any circumstances, perceive or apprehend through any channels except through those of our normal senses. Are we prepared to concede this ?—to imagine that such a wholesale refutation is reasonable or scientific ? I do not think so.

The Ingersoll lecturer at Harvard in 1898 (William James the psychologist) began a brilliant discourse by observing : "The whole subject of immortal life has its prime roots in personal feeling. I have to confess that my own personal feeling about immortality has never been of the keenest order, and that, among the problems that give my mind solicitude, this one does not take the very foremost place." He proceeded to lay down the axiom that thought is a function of the brain ; and he then asked, whether, for this reason, the teaching of immortality was to be rejected. "Most persons," he said, "imbued with what one may call the puritanism of science would feel themselves bound to answer that question with a yes. If any medically or psychologically bred young scientists feel otherwise, it is probably in consequence of that incoherency of mind of which the majority of mankind happily enjoy the privilege. . . . But the more radical and un-compromising disciple of science makes the sacrifice, and, sorrowfully or not, according to his temperament, submits to giving up his hopes of heaven." That was spoken nearly thirty years ago. To-day, it is not "in-coherency of mind" (happy privilege though it be) but science herself who points to a "palpable alterna-tive." James went to the length of claiming the pos-sibility of a function of the brain which was not produc-tive, but transmissive. He conceived that energy from some external source might operate on the brain and direct or enlarge its functional activity. The existence of the individual brain would, we might suppose, modify the stream of spiritual energy as a coloured glass modifies a ray of light. There were thus two available theories : " (1) The brain brings into being the very stuff of consciousness of which our mind consists ; or else (2) Consciousness pre-exists as an entity, and the various brains give to it its various special forms." Of course, the idea of a private soul does not fit in very well with either of these views.

Five years before James delivered his lecture, F. W. H. Myers had written despondently that " the educated world—that part of it, at least, which science leads—is waking up to find that . . . the great hope which inspired their forefathers aforetime is insensibly vanishing away." And he himself could then go no further than to assert that certain cases had convinced him that " the least improbable hypothesis lies in the supposition that some influence on the minds of men on earth is occasionally exercised by the surviving personalities of men departed."

Neither James nor Myers foresaw the enormous possibilities which are contained within the scientific discoveries of the present day : discoveries which have radically changed all previous conceptions of time and of matter, and which have practically demolished the bases of old-fashioned materialism.

While the majority of us, as I have said, are indifferent to the whole question, the more thoughtful very naturally find themselves in a state of suspense. It is not easy for a man to follow the counsel of Maeterlinck, and to form his own particular attitude towards death " in the light of his days and the strength of his intelligence." We are not deeply moved by the prospect of theological heavens and hells, or by the Devachan of theosophy. The non-dimensional consciousness of Buddhism, a concept which is grateful to the imagination and not inacceptable to reason, is too coldly transcendent. " A dialogue between two infants in the womb concerning the state of this world, might handsomely illustrate our ignorance of the next, whereof methinks we yet discourse in Plato's den, and are but embryo philosophers."

That our ignorance is by no means complete is asserted by the churches on the one hand and by those who investigate psychic phenomena on the other. Let us examine the nature of these assertions.

ESCHATOLOGY OF THE CHURCHES

The Christian teaching marked an enormous ethical advance, and at the same time (perhaps incidentally) assured itself of popular support, by proclaiming the spiritual equality of all men, and by thus repudiating the idea of preferential treatment in the after-life. The Christian king and the Christian cobbler might meet in heaven on equal terms, and might be expected to join in mutual discussion of the same heavenly topics. It would all be a question of merit.

In my endeavour to familiarise myself with the Protestant outlook, I have read Bampton lectures, and other theological discourses of the Victorian age—the typical age of Protestantism—but I admit that I have been greatly discouraged by their wordiness and intolerable dullness and vain pomposity. I have been stimulated, however, by the vigorous writing of John Whitley, D.D., Rector of Ballymackey and Chancellor of Killaloe. This good man wrote a book (published in 1846) called *Life Everlasting*, and as we may accept his views as theologically sound, certain passages from this book are herewith, and I hope profitably, transcribed.

" To believe in a future state," wrote the Chancellor of Killaloe, " is an element of our minds—an instinct of nature as well as a dictate of reason." Such belief, moreover, is " a conviction of conscience, known and felt of all men." " There is no such thing as Materia Prima," declares this intrepid scholar, " . . . All things have been created out of nothing." The circumstances of damnation on the one part and beatitude on the other are described with fine declamatory fervour : " When the fire of the last day shall be kindled, and its all-subduing flames shall rage with irresistible force and fury, so that heaven and earth shall be fused and dissolved, whither can such impure carcases of old, unchanged, unrenovated materials, and no better than putrid carrion is now, flee for refuge ? Or how can they endure the all-devouring flames of that universal, everlasting fire that never shall be quenched ? The smoke of their torments, therefore, of necessity ascendeth up for ever and ever. . . . As to the possibility of their dwelling with everlasting burnings, which some have so much doubted : that is the immediate result and consequence of the foulness and impurity of their unrenewed carcases. . . . Have we not in nature, even at present, substances not to be burnt up, nor consumed in the hottest flames ? "

The lot of the righteous, whose physical constitution is evidently of a different kind, is quite another matter : " Animal flesh shall be renewed, rarefied, sublimed into Angel's flesh. . . . The frail, corruptible body, having been dephlegmated from all the lees and filth of mortality, will henceforth be transformed into the winged courser of heaven, the fiery chariot of glory ; exquisitely contrived, and adjusted, to suit the holy tastes, and wishes."

He cannot resist the temptation of reverting to the state of the damned, or of those destined to damnation : a theme in which his powerful but orthodox imagination takes great delight. " The just decree of impartial heaven has adjudged gross, vile, and dreggy bodies to perverted and polluted minds. . . . The body being fumy, vaporous, feculent, they are incapable of

lofty flight. . . . Chained down by the great crassitude
and foul concretions . . . to this low speck, and vile
sink of earth : they can never emerge from its dull
vapours, damp fogs, hazy, misty exhalations." Such
are the fates in store for good souls and for bad souls :
such, in the opinion of Dr. John Whitley and his co-
religionists, are the conditions of immortality for man—
the burning carcase or the fiery chariot. And yet he
admits, that man " is but the last and lowest link in
the long chain of intelligent natures, or rational moral
agents."

Whitley's writing has the double merit of being vivid
and at the same time thoroughly doctrinal. He expresses faithfully the teaching of his church. That teaching is definite enough ; it is neither obscured by meta-
phor nor softened by compassion : if you are damned,
you are very thoroughly and hopelessly and painfully
damned ; and if you are among the blessed you are
nothing less than the " winged courser of heaven."

The eschatology of the Roman Church is, in one respect
at least, a trifle more humane. In an age of strongly
marked social and intellectual discrepancies, such as
ours, the thought of immortality is not without strangeness and terror. The idea that all the stupid people we
see in our daily life, all the unmannerly business men,
all the idiotic girls and affected boys, all the honest
multitudes of the irreproachably correct and the
unspeakably dull—the idea that all these will exist
eternally and recognisably in the next world is one
that might drive a sensitive and intelligent person to
crave total extinction. The thought is not often expressed, but it does exist in the minds of those of superior
standing, manners, and intellect. Here, the Catholic
teaching offers a solution, points to a way out of the
difficulty. There is Purgatory. And we cannot think
of Purgatory without seeing that it is a place where
people are taught better manners, cleansed of their

gross thoughts and awkward habits, and made fit for the company of the elect.

Souls in Purgatory are "benefited by our prayers and good works." The ancient connection between the dead and the living is preserved. Hell is the state or place in which souls are deprived for ever of the Beatific Vision ; and those who die with only original sin on their souls are subjected, not to torment, but to this privation. There are "varying degrees of punishment, corresponding to degrees of guilt." At the last day, or *parousia*, all the dead who are to be judged will rise, the wicked and just alike, with their bodies. "But nothing is defined as to what is required to constitute this identity of the risen and transformed body with the present body." (I quote from the *Catholic Encyclopædia*.) Against the humanity and consideration which characterise so much of the Roman teaching must be set the atrocious condemnation of the souls of unbaptised children, who are ranked with the damned. A point of essential doctrine so savage and so utterly illogical in itself can only be explained on the ground of policy ; a policy having for its aim the speedy enrolment of the children of the devout ; a method of recruiting by terror.

Once the soul is in hell, it is there for ever. Only two have been privileged to leave the place of eternal torment : the soul of the Emperor Trajan, and the soul of Glaoud-ar-Skanv, a native of Brittany. The first was indebted to the intercession of Pope Gregory, and the second to the prayers of his mother.

The teaching of the Koran does not differ greatly from that of the Christian churches. At death, the body becomes earth, and the soul enters on a state of sleep or unconsciousness. Soul and body are reunited on the judgment day. On that day, the great records are unrolled before God and His angels ; the good enter the fields of Paradise, and the evil are cast into Jahannam.

Church doctrines have been devised and sanctioned

at sundry times and by sundry councils, in accordance with ecclesiastical policy or in response to social pressure. We are now taught, by eminent divines, that the church takes a pride in her " mobility." That is equivalent to saying that her sheep insist on doctrinal concessions, and on a share in the control of her rites and services. It so comes about that it is extremely difficult to state definitely what are and what are not the essential doctrines. In the case of the Protestant Church, it is impossible to make any such statement. Rome has a firmer discipline because she rules, in spiritual matters, over races who are naturally indolent, devout, and submissive ; and because her organisation has always been in the hands of supremely intelligent men. The doctrine of eternal punishment is of statutory importance to all Christian churches, together with the doctrine of eternal felicity. That the dead are judged, privately at death and publicly at the last day, is an essential doctrine. Those who are damned are flung into hell immediately after their death ; but as the ultimate result of good and of bad actions can only be known at the end of the world, a final judgment is necessary in order that each soul may receive perfect justice. The last judgment, therefore, serves two purposes : (1) it passes sentence on human actions in view of their effectual conclusion, (2) it proves to all concerned, simultaneously, the justice of each individual sentence.

In regard to the nature of the soul and the constitution of the spiritual body, the churches have no official teaching whatsoever.

PSYCHIC RESEARCH

At the present day, an attempt has been made to rediscover the soul, and to make it respectable in the eyes of science. Although the attempt has not succeeded in its main object (for the soul remains absolutely beyond the reach of scientific demonstration) it has not been without result. It has brought comfort to the credulous, notoriety to the vulgar, and a considerable degree of self-esteem to the ignorant. Moreover, it has greatly assisted the sales of our penny papers. But, in its more serious aspects, it must be admitted that it has achieved something worthier. It has recorded phenomena which reveal the supra-normal activities of the human organism, and which merit our close attention. In our contempt for the fools and impostors who, though for such different reasons, are attracted by this enquiry, we must not forget that psychic research counts among its advocates and practitioners men of the most advanced mental calibre and of first-rate scientific endowment. In many cases, these men, though they have failed to convince the world, claim to have found conviction themselves. Such conviction is unquestionably dependent on idiosyncratic tendencies; it is not a conviction which can be demonstrated (as Flammarion thought) or stated in terms of positive language; it cannot be proved by experiment.

Before a man is ready to consider the question of his immortality he has to decide whether there is any part of him, any personal or personally conscious part, which is capable of existing under conditions that are totally independent of, and distinct from, the conditions of bodily existence. When once animation has ceased, the body as a sensory apparatus is finished with, absolutely and finally. There is no doubt of that. The death of the body is the end of the individual, in so far as the individual is conditioned by the nature and restrictions of the body and of the senses. Is there anything left? Is there another form of the individual; a form which is not conditioned by the limitations of organic life? Mind, if there is anything left, we need not ask ourselves whether it can be seen or weighed. Thought is neither visible nor ponderable; neither is energy. If, therefore, there is any part of the human personality which survives death, we need not take for granted that we should be able to see it with our eyes, or that we should be able to determine its weight and dimensions. But we may very well assume that a surviving personality must possess an enormous degree of some kind of force. A form of energy which can hold together the human personality in a disembodied state, even for a time, should be distinctly perceptible to the embodied consciousness. To the higher consciousness, or to the senses? We have to make a distinction. We know that there are certain transmissions which appear to touch the higher centres directly, without the intervention of the senses : these may be referred to the senses, and given the semblance of visible, auditional, or tangible form, but apparently they are not received directly by sensory means. A familiar instance of this is to be found in that vague mental uneasiness which is the premonition of danger or sickness or death, and particularly of some tragedy affecting a distant friend. That such uneasiness does correspond with a distant event has been frequently proved. Obviously, the senses, as we understand them, have nothing to do with impressions of this kind. They are psychic ; that is, they pertain to agencies which are not conditioned by the ordinary limitations of the senses ; they possess actually a power which thought seems to possess—a power which acts independently of time, space, or mass. Now, if these impressions—call them premonitions, or what you will—really do exist, if the transference of thought or emotion from one individual to another without the intervention of the senses really does occur, if the mind is really able to perceive events which take place beyond the range of physical perceptivity (and we believe that we have proof of the authenticity of these phenomena) then we may be justified in assuming that the personality may exist under conditions which

are in no way related to the conditions of the bodily life.
Can we go further ; can we affirm that it does actually
so exist ?

The transference of thought or of mental impressions
from one mind to another, or the appearance of the
phantasm of a living person, does not necessarily imply
the conscious participation of the agent : i.e. of the
person whose actual image or thoughts present themselves to some other person who is at a distance. Such
transference, in fact, is more often than not accom-
plished, not only without the volition of the agent, but
without his knowledge. In other words, the personal
consciousness of the agent need not come into play at
all. If these phenomena occur during the lifetime of
the agent, absolutely without reference to what we term
his personal consciousness, is it necessary to assume that
similar phenomena, which appear to originate from the
personality of a defunct person, are associated with
a conscious state ? May they not be due to an impersonal
continuance of the mental or psychic elements ?—mere
automatism ? It may be that we are too ready to connect
personality with consciousness. It may be that consciousness, like a kind of sensitised ether, flows everywhere, and that its manifestation in a human personality
is only a dissolving manifestation—a temporary con-
centration of greater or lesser density. It may be that,
in accordance with the greater or lesser receptivity of
the human vessel, a greater or lesser share of this consciousness is contained within it ; but, just as the
breaking of a vessel may spill but not destroy what it
contains, so the death of the human body need not
imply the immediate dispersal or destruction of its
conscious contents. (It must be understood that I am
using the term consciousness in place of a concept for
which we have no actual word.) But it is not necessary
to assume that the surviving form of these conscious
contents is personal, in the restricted sense of the term ;

any more than it is necessary to assume that the contents of a thing, when separated from it, can be regarded as the thing itself. It is, perhaps, the recognition of this possibility which has induced certain religions to lay stress on the importance of bodily resurrection : the reunion of vessel and contents, and hence the restoration of complete personality. It may be that without this reunion of body and soul (an impossible reunion, it seems) the personality can never be restored. After death, perchance, the individual's share of consciousness, gradually disintegrating, passes into the general stream. The ghost, in fact, may be an aspect, not of survival, but of decomposition.

There is another great problem. If the human personality survives death, since when has it survived ? Does that survival date, so to speak, from a given stage in the physical and psychical evolution of a given animal ? Are there degrees of completeness in survival ? Does the consciousness of other animals survive in an individual form ? It is generally assumed that there is some connection between the soul and the thinking part of man ; but it must not be forgotten that we differ mentally from other animals in degree only, not in kind. Essentially, we do not differ at all.

Psychic research has not found the answers to these and to the other questions, and it seems probable that the answers will never be found by living men. But, as I have said, psychic research has rendered valuable service in proving the authenticity of certain phenomena.

The first serious experiments in thought-transference, which led to such remarkable developments, were carried out in the 'seventies by Professor Barrett ; and the subject was taken up by Lodge (now Sir Oliver) in 1883. The investigation of psychic phenomena has been seriously undertaken, within the last forty years, by a number of brilliant men, such as Lodge, Crookes, Myers, Gurney, Sidgwick, Lombroso, Flammarion, and

Richet. Whether they are all equally convincing, or whether any of them are convincing, the opinions and the experiments of these investigators are entitled to respect. They are the opinions and experiments of men of the highest scientific repute. They stand in a very different category from that which includes the lucubrations of novelists, advertisement-writers, silly ladies, and neurotic clergymen.

It may be said, I think, that our knowledge of the superficial or apparent nature of certain phenomena is now well established. As regards monitions of a visible kind (the apparition of a living or a dead person, desirous of conveying information or warning) we know that these are of varying opacity. Sometimes the features are distinct ; at others they are blurred or filmy. A voice is but rarely associated with these phantoms, and they are generally impalpable. The length of the period between the appearance of the phantom and the occurrence of the event with which it is supposed to be connected is variable. Myers says that nearly all cases of phantoms appearing before death are related to cases of illness, not of accident or of sudden demise. Where the death has been swift or violent, the apparition is usually retarded. The duration of the full visibility of these apparitions is very short : a few seconds, or at most a minute or two. It is considered by Richet that those which are seen simultaneously by several persons are certainly objective, that they occupy a position in space ; but this may be doubted, especially in view of the fact that the same apparition may be seen at the same moment by persons in different places. Occasionally these monitions take a symbolic form. Thus Mme. A. dreams that there is a ring at the door : the parlourmaid enters with the startling announcement, " Madame, it is Death." Mme. A. then sees a coffin, and in it the body of a friend, of whose decease (which had actually occurred) she was then ignorant (Richet). So also, Mrs.

H. D. dreams that she sees a friend of hers, Maria, playing chess with Dr. D., but wearing a thick black veil. Mrs. D. makes a remark about the veil, and Maria answers, " It is because I am dead " ; she then raises the veil, disclosing the face of a skull, with hollow eye-sockets (Flammarion). Maria, previously in robust health, died the same night.

Monitory apparitions, such as these, are often seen in dreams, and we may not be wrong in concluding that they are always subjective, and not connected in any way with materialisation. An apparition, of course, is not invariably present. A voice may be heard. You are at the theatre, when a voice in your ear says : " Go home quickly." You obey, and find that you are just in time to prevent a serious outbreak of fire, though no one knew of the peril. Whence comes the warning in such a case ? By an extension of your own percep-tions, it may be, you have become aware of what was happening, and you have given yourself an apparently audible signal. No one else hears the voice.

Chevreul gives an extraordinary case of a monition in which there is no actual appearance. Two men named Baeschly, father and son, are alone in a house at Saverne. Towards midnight they are awakened from their sleep by loud noises, as though doors are being slammed. They seek in vain for the cause, and at length discover that the front door is wide open. Three times they shut and lock the door, and three times it bursts open ; and at last they tie it with rope. In due course a letter arrives from America, relating the death of Baeschly's brother, who, just before he died, had said : " I have been on a long journey ; I have paid a visit to my brother."

We have innumerable stories of sounds, and even of the movement of objects, preceding the news of a death. According to Le Braz, such things are of frequent occur-rence in Brittany ; and there the people hear mutterings or whispers, the shifting of planks, hammering, the creaking and whining of cart-wheels, and heavy blows struck upon the door. The story of the " dancing peas " is a very singular one : An old woman who kept a village shop, growing feeble, employed a young girl as assistant. One day, while the old woman was lying a-bed, a peasant came to the shop to buy peas. The girl placed them in the dish of the scales, when, as though furiously animated, they all began to dance and jump about, to the amazement both of vendor and purchaser. After the peasant had left, though hesitating to buy bewitched peas, the girl ran to tell the old woman ; and found that she was dead. Then we have the story of a woman seeing the severed head of her son rolling on the kitchen table : he had been decapitated through an accident on board ship—the snapping of a steel hawser, or something of the sort—and the head had rolled on the moving deck before the sailors could get hold of it and pick it up. Three separate visions are recorded in the case of one death : A young girl saw the funeral cortège of her uncle before his death ; then, sitting with others to watch the dying man, she saw a coffin brought by invisible hands into the room : on the day of the actual funeral she was sent on her rounds with the hand-cart, delivering milk ; meeting the cortège (the real one this time) she hid in the hedge while it passed, and saw the ghost of the dead man following the procession.

Similar stories, narrated by people of learning and culture, as well as by peasants, come to the notice of everyone, and are recorded by the thousand. As a good example, I will quote a typical instance, of the symbolic kind, from Richet : Charles Demay, a professor at Dijon, saw a colleague, G., in Paris, who made a request which he (Demay) could not agree to, and left him in a state of extreme agitation. Two nights later, Demay, being then at a distance of 210 miles from Paris, dreamt that he was in a boat on the Seine. He trailed his hand in the water, and it was seized by a fish ; the head of the fish, raised by his hand from the water, suddenly changed to the countenance of G. The dreamer woke, and noted that the time was 2.20 a.m. The dream was related to G's sister, and afterwards it was learnt that G. had leaped into the river on the night of the dream, and that his body had been taken out by the police at 2.30 a.m.

The celebrated Storie case, one of the best in Myers' collection, is very remarkable. It is another instance of the monitory dream. Mrs. Storie, in Hobart, 1874, dreamt, four hours after the accident had occurred, that her brother had been killed. The dream was unusual ; it consisted of a series of half-symbolic visions, the meaning of which was explained by a ghostly voice. Actually the brother had been killed on the railway line : he had apparently fallen asleep on the track, and the top of his head had been struck off by some projection, perhaps a footboard on a passing train. The news reached Mrs. Storie a week later. It is possible, of course, to question her veracity, but Myers and others regarded the evidence as good, and the character of her own account is strongly in favour of its acceptance. Perhaps the most notable feature in this case is the fact that the accident was not known to any living person until the morning following its occurrence : it was not observed by the driver of the train or by anyone else.

Richet, having studied an immense number of these cases, makes the following conclusive observation : " It is . . . well established that at the moment of death some vibration takes place, actuating something in nature, which occasionally gives information of the death to those who are sensitive." And he adds, " . . . most probably the vision itself is a hallucinatory symbol."

The most amazing experiment recorded by Richet was

reported by Dr. Dufay. A prisoner in the jail at Blois strangled himself with his necktie. Dufay obtained this necktie and put a piece of it in a folded paper which he handed, without comment, to a medium named Marie. She described the material, and told how the man had taken his life. Then she proceeded to explain that the prisoner had been charged with murder (which was correct) ; that he had, indeed, committed this murder ; and that he had killed his victim with a hatchet. The hatchet, she said, would be found in such-and-such a place, where it had been thrown away. It was, in fact, actually found, afterwards, in the place described. We may call this " pragmatic cryptesthesia " or " a sensibility to emanations from things," but the true meaning of such a phenomenon is at present beyond our grasp. We ask ourselves whether the poor heathen, who believes that the ghostly essence of a man clings to his garments, is not just as near the truth as we are.

Camille Flammarion, the great French astronomer, who has recently died, collected and classified many hundreds of documents relating to psychical experience. He convinced himself of the survival of the human spirit. Religions, he said, were no longer acceptable from the philosophic point of view, though they might still be of use, and he believed that men should turn to science for the new revelation of spiritual truth. Although he recorded a number of well-attested cases, his eagerness predisposed him to accept as evidential certain statements of very questionable value. It was enough for him that a correspondent should introduce himself in this manner : " Je suis un homme bien portant, âgé de 47 ans, à la taille droite et haute, avec embonpoint modéré, ayant bonne mine, bon appetit, et bon sommeil, ancien employé de l'administration des lignes tele-graphiques—et libre-penseur." The story of an appari-tion follows ; and Flammarion observes gravely : " D'après la description de l'auteur sur sa propre

personne, il serait difficile d'admettre ici une hallucination, une impression nerveuse, une illusion imaginaire."
From the nature of things, it is inevitable that the
majority of the documents in such a collection must
fail to convince. But the ensemble, the categorical
presentation of these documents, does produce an effect.
Indeed, it is not too much to say, that no intelligent
man who reads these letters and statements with an
unbiassed mind, even if he only accepts a minority as
communicated in good faith, is any longer in a position
to deny the possibility of survival.

Flammarion's great argument in favour of the existence of a personal soul or spirit is contained in his
axiom : " It is not the eye that sees : it is not the
brain that thinks." He believes that the brain itself
is not the initial cause of thought : the cerebral processes
are effects, not causes. But this argument does not offer
conclusive proof, even if its premises are admitted.
Thought, like optical vision, may be the result of the
brain reacting to external stimuli.

An apparent communication from, or a vision of,
a person who has been dead for some little time, does
not necessarily involve the theory of survival. Mental
impressions are often retained in a latent form before
they emerge on the level of the consciousness ; and the
vision or communication may have been transferred to
the mind of the percipient while the agent was yet
living. This idea of latency is, indeed, compatible with
Flammarion's own teaching : " Ce n'est pas la rétine
qui est frappé par une réalité affective, ce sont les
couches optiques du cerveau qui sont excitées par une
force psychique." It is by no means necessary, therefore, to assume " a dynamism continuing the personality." But the cases defined by Myers as those of
" deflected perception " are exceedingly strange. In
these cases, the manifestation is not perceived at all by
the person who is most likely to be concerned, but by

some stranger or servant, by some one who is in no way
interested in the " ghost," and who has never seen him,
or heard about him, while he was in the flesh. But even
here, objective reality need not be assumed ; the psychic
impression may have originated in the subconscious
mind of the person who was acquainted with the " ghost,"
and it may have passed thence to the conscious level of
some other mind. For all that, we must remember what
is too frequently forgotten by the average enquirer :
an event which is neither apprehended nor registered
by scientific means, nor readily explained by scientific
deduction, may be none the less a real event. Science
reveals, not the extent of our knowledge, but the extent
of our ignorance. And, moreover, the hypothesis of survival, even if it is only a hypothesis, does offer, in many
cases, the simplest and most workable explanation.

Although the literature dealing with psychic matters
has now reached formidable dimensions (so formidable,
that a large book-shop entirely devoted to the sale of
this literature has recently been opened in London),
Myers's great work on *Human Personality*, published in
1903, still remains the most complete and scholarly
treatise on the subject. Myers believed that he could
only account for certain phenomena by assuming that
the disembodied human spirit was able to influence the
minds of the living. In his own words : " . . . it
seems to me now that the evidence for communication
with the spirits of identified deceased persons through
the trance-utterings and writings of sensitives apparently
controlled by those spirits is established beyond serious
attack." And again : " I hold that certain manifestations of certain individualities, associated now or formerly with certain definite organisms, have been observed
in operation apart from those organisms, both while
the organisms were still living, and after they had decayed." It is easy to doubt, easy to produce alternative
explanations ; yet we cannot lightly dismiss the con-

sidered words of one of the most brilliant intellects of modern times.

The majority of men have refused to accept as proof of survival the utterances of the medium or the writings of the planchette. At the same time, we may well ask : is it possible to imagine any sort of ideal proof ? Is it possible to devise any sort of ideal experiment ? There would always be another explanation : an explanation based on the dim apprehension, the imperfect knowledge of the powers and faculties of something which is fully as little understood, as mysterious and evasive as the soul itself—the human mind.

It is, indeed, to the service which it has rendered in exploring human faculties that we are indebted to psychic research. The most that can be admitted without reserve in regard to its exploration of the spiritual realm is, that it has given a certain plausibility to the following hypotheses : (a) manifestations, apparently originating from a living personality, may be perceived at a distance by means of some faculty which is extra to what we term the normal faculties ; (b) exactly similar manifestations, apparently originating from the spirit of a deceased person, are perceived in a like manner ; (c) an operative essence of the personality seems to adhere to personal belongings, such as clothes or trinkets. The fact which is certainly established is, that there are perceptive faculties which are immeasurably wider in range than those which are dependent on the ordinary senses.

Thus it will be seen, that the investigators of psychic phenomena find themselves, after a great deal of trouble, in the position which primitive man assumes with no trouble at all. A prodigious amount of intellectual effort and of tireless application has led to conclusions which are identical with those of the careless savage.

GHOSTS

Among civilised nations, the belief in ghosts is maintained stoutly by the peasants, less positively affirmed by the middle classes, and generally repudiated by those who imagine that they possess a superior education. But it may be doubted whether the most indurated sceptic is proof against an occasional surreptitious and unavowed tremor. To a greater or lesser extent, we all believe in ghosts. Even those who proclaim most loudly that there are no such things have their sudden misgivings and anxious moments.

Modern ghosts differ but little from the " *senex macie et squalore confectus* " of Pliny the Younger : there is, in fact, a sameness in the greater number of our traditional or popular ghost stories. Although religion and science have both dealt with apparitions of the dead, each in its own fashion, the popular belief continues unchanged, and a number of ghosts are seen every year by people who are fully as reasonable and respectable as their neighbours. If we sum up the whole matter in that attractive word " hallucination," we have yet to explain how it is that the one hallucination of a lifetime, or the rare hallucinations of one who is not subject to mental disturbance, should take this peculiar form. It is true that the apparition is generally that of a person who has been well known to the seer : therefore the image is already stored in the mind, and there is no difficulty in assuming that this image may be externalised when the necessary conditions are present. But that does not apply to every case, though perhaps it does to the majority of those which have survived examination.

Let us see how the belief in ghosts is manifested by different kinds of people in modern Europe.

First, let us consider briefly the political value of the ghost, Those who are foolish enough, or brave enough, or merely unfortunate enough, to be slain in a political quarrel, a noisy insurrection, or some popular tumult, acquire peculiar greatness. The ghost is not allowed to admit defeat. Full advantage is taken of his usefulness as a propagandist, if not as a still active member of the party for whose rights he was so zealous while he lived in the body. There is no rest for the martyr : he is the recipient of continual prayers and importunities, and he is dragged willy-nilly into the wars and dissensions of his clique. The value of cultus as a party asset was realised during the recent disturbances in Ireland : indeed, those who die voluntarily or by accident in the defence of an idea or of a nation impart a tremendous momentum to the cause for which they have lost their lives. In war, where every dead soldier, by virtue of being dead, becomes a powerful moral force, present alike on the field of battle and in the councils of State, the cult of the immortal fallen is carefully fostered. The military ghost is always credited with the most bloodthirsty sentiments towards his former enemies ; so much so, that the idea of any of those enemies visiting his (the ghost's) country in time of restored peace is supposed to fill him with indignation— until, like any ordinary man, he acquires a new sense of the national interest. Every politician knows the political value of a statesman's funeral, especially if the statesman's party is in a precarious condition. Thus, to the soldier, the patriot, the politician, the protectionist, and the revolutionary, ghosts are very real, and of much importance.

Myers defined a ghost as " a manifestation of persistent personal energy." That manifestation is nowhere more persistent and nowhere more energetic than among the peasants of Brittany ; though the belief in ghosts is a characteristic of the Keltic remnant in general. Every dead person, say the Bretons, has to return three times. The *revenant* may appear in seeming solidity, as though he had never died at all. (An Irish

belief also.) There is a farm in Kermaria-Sulard where
the deceased farmer and his wife both returned after
burial, and set about their business, the one in the house
and the other in the fields. The property was then in
other hands, but that made no difference to the *revenants*;
the woman washed the dishes and baked the cakes, and
smiled pleasantly at her successor, while the man helped
with the ploughing. But there is no story which equals
in strangeness and in sheer horror the story of the old
man of Keranniou, as told by Le Braz. The old man
(a farmer) came back after his death, and plagued his
relatives and neighbours with malicious and terrible
persistence. At times he was visible, at times he was
only felt. He filled the house with loud sound ; he
was riotous and took delight in cruel horse-play. His
presence was accepted, at length, as that of a living
person, and he was familiarly known as Le Vieux. If
a man was knocked down by an unexpected blow on the
head, he would see, as he picked himself up, the grinning
face, and hear the malignant laughter of Le Vieux.
If there was a sudden thunder in the skittle-alley, it was
Le Vieux playing his game. His final and most hideous
escapade was to beget a child on his widow : a sickly
infant, with no eyes, but with abnormal intelligence.
Le Vieux was constantly found at the child's cradle,
which he rocked with a heavy hand, jerking it roughly
back and forth, yet seeming to regard the baby with
a kind of ferocious affection. The child, fully endowed
with speech, and appearing to see with its hollow sockets,
died when it was seven months old. Le Vieux followed
the body to the graveyard, and was seen no more.
We have also a story of a dead lover coming back for
his betrothed and carrying her away on a horse—
a real horse. Next morning the grave-diggers find her
body, horribly crushed and broken, lying at the bottom
of the grave which had been dug for the man.

These are grim stories. They reveal the ghost in one

of his most terrible aspects : indeed, the term ghost hardly applies in its ordinary sense ; though we have no equivalent for the more exact term of *revenant*.

From one of his peasant informants, Le Braz obtained a story which corresponds closely with many of the " authenticated " cases recorded in the annals of psychic research. Three persons were sitting up to watch the dead body of *le vicaire*. The body was in a chair, clothed in fine vestments, and it seemed as if the dead man was looking about him with complacency and benevolence. Presently, two of the watchers heard the chiming of a distant bell, and then a sound of music filled the room ; and afterwards came a noise like that of myriads of swarming bees, at times loud and sonorous and at times confused and faint. The third watcher, though fully awake, heard nothing at all. Such cases are not infrequent. A sound of music, of voices, is heard soon after a death has taken place ; it is heard clearly by some of those who are present and not heard by others. Although this is not, properly speaking, a ghost story, it deals with a phenomenon connected with the death-chamber, and one which has been observed, so it appears, by simple villagers as well as by folk of learning and culture.

It must be admitted that, with the exception of folk-lore, the best ghost stories are those which are purely imaginary. Books which profess to describe authentic apparitions are usually made up of loose, inchoate material. The writers give us the trivial facts of their social life ; they tell us that " the Duchess was a keen bridge player and took a lively interest in ghosts," they introduce us to the silly tittle-tattle of Riviera hotels, and they explain why it was that their great-grandfathers were not decorated at the battle of Water-loo. We are told, perhaps, that mediums should not indulge in black coffee. Then, after learning the topo-graphy of the " astral plane," we are informed that the ghosts of pet cats have been frequently observed by sensitives. There is much harm, I think, in such books, for they bring into disrepute what should be a matter for cool and intelligent enquiry, and the ridicule which they naturally provoke has the effect of making the average person fight shy of the whole subject ; and in this enquiry the testimony of the average person is of the first importance.

Why is it that no true ghost story has ever been well related ? That apparitions should only be seen by the flighty or the illiterate is hardly credible. I cannot explain this. I can only state, with regret, that no person of high intelligence has yet given us a good first-hand authentic ghost story.

There is no doubt that we discover a gradual thinning-out of the belief in ghosts as we move from the ruder to the more civilised grades of society. To the peasant the ghost is very real ; to the middle-class man he is a problem. The out-and-out sceptic need not concern us, in this or in any other matter. The existence of the ghost, or of some surviving form of the personality which is closely in touch with human affairs, is assumed for a variety of reasons and purposes. In honouring or exploiting the sacred memory of the dead, men honour or exploit something which they are willing to regard as alive ; something which is able to reciprocate the sentiments of the embodied living and to respond to their wishes.

FUNERALS, MONUMENTS, AND EPITAPHS

Although a funeral is ostensibly an occasion for the public display of sorrow, it still serves a more archaic purpose. We behave at a funeral in such a way that the dead person may be favourably impressed by our conduct, and gratified by perceiving our doleful demeanour. Hence we put on inconceivably ugly clothes, and hire a most hideous equipage, in order that our frien d may be carried to his grave in the correct manner. This we do, not to show respect to the dead body—for a dead body is a useless and horrible thing—but to show respect to something which we are inclined to think of as still associated with the body. That is why most of us are careful to raise our hats when we meet a funeral cortège. That is why it is considered unlucky, by peasants, to look at a funeral procession through a window : if you do this, the ghost, who is in the procession, thinks you are mocking him ; he thinks you are saying, " Aha ! here am I all snug in the house, while you are shut up in that ugly box." That is why certain people (of slightly deranged mentality) will spend the whole of a winter's night shivering in the street, so that they may witness the passing of some beloved personage. In short, that is why the dead body of a man is often treated with greater respect than the man himself received while he was alive.

It may have been some kind of uneasy recognition of this pagan element in funerals which induced the Quakers to eschew all forms of obsequial splendour. No sentiment of any sort was shown by these austere people, either in the dress which they wore at funerals, or in the manner of the burial. Their graves were dug in plain, orderly rows, neither was one distinguished from another. They abhorred monuments, and held that epitaphs were vain, worldly, and foolish. In no way did they exhibit their sorrow by any symbol or decoration.

Monumental inscriptions are also designed for an archaic purpose. The departed are, or were, praised in terms of the most absurd flattery, and at the same time we hasten to remind ourselves that they are " at rest," " lost to sight "—disposed of in such a way that we shall see no more of them ; we shall not be terrified by their reappearance. They have become sacred memories.

" The writer of an epitaph," said Dr. Johnson, " should

not be considered as saying nothing but what is strictly
true. Allowance must be made for some degree of exaggerated praise. In lapidary inscriptions a man is not
upon oath." Formerly, it was not unusual to celebrate
the departed with an astonishing degree of " exaggerated praise." As an example of this, take the epitaph
of Mr. Robert Hughes, Philomath, of Flint : " Sun,
Moon, and Stars ! all ye etherial host, Condole the Death
of him with whom ye boast Ye correspondence held ! "
The heavens themselves are called on to remember
their indebtedness to Mr. Robert Hughes. Equally
bombastic is the epitaph written for Henry VII, which
describes him as " the Glory of Monarchy and Light of
the World." The less tremendous but more lovable
qualities of private worth found ample record in the
epitaphs of the eighteenth century. Let me choose two
of these, to illustrate the attitude of our forefathers
towards their defunct relatives. Mrs. Jessop, a clergy-
man's widow, died in 1737. She was described on her
tomb as " A woman of exemplary Piety, Charity, and all
other Christian Graces ; An Ornament to the Church of
England. She was always a great lover of Neatness,
without much regard to Mode or Fashion ; and, though
she kept as close at Home as if confined to a Cloister,
no one better understood good-breeding (if what goes
by that Name be real Benevolence) expressed in the most
obliging Manner." Dr. Hugh Chamberlain was buried in
Westminster Abbey. His epitaph, after relating his
skill as a physician and accoucheur, proceeds thus :
" He had so delicate a Taste for the Elegancies of Life,
was endowed with so exalted a Spirit, so munificent a
Disposition, and was blessed with a Person so graceful,
that you could not help believing that he had some noble
Author for his Origin ; and, indeed, you may trace his
Family Four Hundred Years, in a gradual ascent to
the ancient Earls of TANKERVILLE."
Warrior's tombs of the same period often record

great deeds of arms, and exhort the readers to emulate them. Thus, on the monument of that sturdy old fighter, Admiral Boscawen, we read : " Even after Death, BOSCAWEN'S Triumphs shall to succeeding Ages stand a fair Example, and rouse the active Sons of Britain, like him, to dart the Terror of their Thunders on Gallic Perfidy ! "

We cannot, it seems, rid our minds of the idea that a deceased person remains in some way connected with his monument, or with any image or representation of him. For this reason, a monument which deviates from the anthropomorphic tradition is certain to provoke hostility. The public has always believed that a man should be commemorated by his own image or by the accepted symbol of his faith. If they are shown something which is illustrative of his genius, or something which is manifestly a work of genius in itself, but which does not actually represent the deceased in the traditional manner, they are moved by an extraordinary impulse of indignation. It is for this reason that respectable though silly men, who know no more about art or genius than my cat does, become positively demented if they are shown a memorial which, in their opinion, lacks the proper sense of commemoration. The proper way of commemorating an illustrious man, in the eyes of the said respectable men, is to set up an image of him, an image of unmistakable likeness, in some hard and weatherproof substance. Everyone can understand that. It is a *ka*-figure. The spirit of the man is willingly associated with his effigy ; but how can it be associated with a decorative panel which it cannot possibly understand, and which means nothing to the ordinary person ? So the old cult persists : the cult of the ghost and the cult of the image, of man and of the likeness of man.

The modern attitude towards the dead and towards the doctrine of immortality is by no means a simple one.

(In speaking of the modern attitude, I mean that of the average thoughtful man ; not that of the merely average man.) While the problem of immortality has not been solved, either by religion or by psychic research, or by the established sciences, the teaching of materialism has been rudely shaken, if not completely destroyed, by the discovery that we are as yet most imperfectly acquainted with the properties of matter. Although conviction may flash upon certain individuals as the result of a sudden mental disturbance, or, shall we say ? of a revelation, it is not within the reach of the majority. It cannot be transmitted from one person to another. It is not self-evident, neither is it demonstrable. Perhaps agnosticism is the most prepared and reasonable attitude. Even those who are religious (priests themselves, indeed) admit that they cannot accept the teaching of the churches. Spiritualism, though the value of its serious achievement in demonstrating supra-normal faculties is in no way lessened by the folly and credulity of the ignorant people who are duped by spurious phenomena, has failed entirely to prove its case. It has, indeed, proved nothing which does not come more properly within the domain of psychology.

Death presents, to each one of us, a personal and particular, it need not be a terrifying, problem. It is not altogether without profit to reflect on the plain, untroubled conviction of earlier or more primitive races ; on the calmness with which death has been faced already by innumerable millions of men.

CHAPTER VII

CONCLUSION

OUR enquiry has shown us that, in the ancient or primitive stages of society, men are unanimous in believing that the human spirit is immortal. The soul is not necessarily regarded as a single, indivisible entity. The belief that the spiritual part of man exists and survives in more than one form is a widespread belief. Social conduct is not regarded as having any bearing on the future life of the soul, until a somewhat advanced level of culture has been reached.

Immortality is not invariably thought of as unconditional, still less as an eternal state. In some places, only gentlemen have immortal souls : in others, only the spirits of the extremely powerful survive.

That the spiritual essence of a man is mysteriously diffused and projected, so that it clings to his property or clothes, to the places he has frequented, and, above all, to any fragment of his body, is a very general idea.

The dead body itself is usually looked on as the centre of strong and dangerous energies—energies which are partly intrinsic and partly derived from contact with the surrounding spiritual elements. Only in exceptional instances is it treated with indifference. Its preservation and its ceremonial destruction are both carried out in accordance with the teachings in regard to the welfare of the ghost. Either it is of great sanctity, as the residence of the soul or of some aspect of the surviving personality, or it is a carnal encumbrance from which the dependent spirit has to be set free. At first glance, it seems as if the conservation of the body was the more ancient practice, though the observances of extremely primitive folk, such as the Australians, prevent us from asserting this as a positive fact.

There is no such thing as a primitive form of scepticism. To primitive man, souls, or at least certain elect souls, survive the death of the body. We have seen that his ideas regarding the future life of the soul vary in the most amazing manner. But there is no doubt that he regards a future life, of some sort, as unquestionable. Whether he looks forward to that life with satisfaction is not clear ; but it is certain that he is continually disturbed by the thought of those of his fellows who have already entered upon it. At best, the imagined presence of those who have gone before fills him with uneasiness ; at worst, with frantic terror. He does not seem to derive consolation from the fact that his own turn is coming. Occasionally, as death approaches, he may exercise a sort of tyranny over his companions ; but that is induced rather by their quickening fears than by his own sensation of power. The testimony of primitive man in regard to the souls of the dead reveals the fact that he looks on them with a greater or lesser degree of apprehension. If his attitude towards them shows, at times, a seeming affection, that affection is of an incidental and transient nature.

Civilised man, while ceasing to retain the ancient fear of disembodied spirits, in any avowed form, ceases also to believe implicitly in their existence ; his affection towards the deceased is, for the most part, of a purely memorial character. He professes to honour the memory of the dead rather than the dead themselves. This is largely due to the growth of theology. Instead of being an essential part of the social texture, as it is in all primitive societies, religion has withdrawn from, or has been crowded out of, the complex scheme of civilised life. Limited, it may be, by the very development of his reason, man has a tendency to accept as true only those phenomena which come within the range of ordinary observation, and which respond to the conditions of ordinary experiment. Although he now perceives that he is only beginning to realise dimly the nature and potentiality of matter, he still believes that the ultimate test of truth is the test of tangibility, of apprehension by the physical senses, whether directly or with the assistance of scientific apparatus. Such a position is, of course, proved untenable by the results of its own achievement. In his desire to show that he is guided solely by reason, man is being defeated by his chosen ally : reason, by a final and brilliant exertion, has proved its own fallibility.

It so comes about that the majority of us find ourselves, as regards the problem of survival, in an indeterminate state, neither convinced nor disabused. Probably we should welcome conviction ; but we are not able to accept the arguments, either of the priest or of the person who investigates psychic phenomena—I hesitate to say of the scientist.

The question which comes naturally into our minds after an examination of the evidence relating to primitive forms of belief is this : In separating ourselves from the primitive outlook (or in assuming that we have done so, or that we ought to do so), are we rejecting an empty superstition, or are we rejecting a truth of the very highest importance ? If our senses are in every way more acute than those of the savage, how is it that we fail to perceive what he is so confident of perceiving ?

It is true that the cult of the dead, howbeit in a restrained and often disguised form, is present among civilised nations. But it exists, where the greater number is concerned, in what I must term automatic forms. It may be argued that it still lingers as other forms of primitive thought linger, as superstition lingers. Moreover, it is not always a surviving though enfeebled cult, but a thriving convention which asserts itself.

A man does not soon marry after the death of his wife, not because he fears her ghost, but because he fears the opinion of his children or his neighbours. Most men would admit that they uncover their heads before a tomb, a cenotaph, or a dead body, not because they feel that they are being watched by the jealous dead, but in order that they may not appear lacking in good manners. We may ask, however, why these gestures should be regarded as good manners. For whose attention or benefit are these good manners displayed? It must be admitted, that certain observances in connection with the veneration of the dead are not to be explained by the statement that they are purely conventional; observances which, as we saw in the preceding chapter, seem to have preserved much of their primitive meaning.

Thus, no conclusion is possible. But the intelligent man, even if he is unable to form a definite opinion in regard to these matters, may at least take up a composed attitude. Perhaps he will be led to think that the evidence preponderates in favour of the truth of survival. Perhaps he will seek refuge, if not peace, in the mechanistic point of view—or in what is left of it. Perhaps he will decide that a resolute agnosticism, a deference to all possibilities, is safer in the long run, even if less spectacular for the present. What we know is so little : what we may know is so vast. Elated by our very imperfect control of matter, we fail to appreciate the possibility of matter and spirit being one and the same thing.

That a great truth is discovered through some mistake, and not apprehended in its essential aspect, makes it neither more nor less the truth. Primitive man looks on a flash of lightning as the spear of some offended god, and I look on it as a discharge of electrical force ; but we both see the lightning. A savage, if he dreams of a dead person, tells me that he has actually seen that person ; while I maintain that he has merely experienced a psychological disturbance of a purely subjective character : but whether the souls of the dead do or do not survive, or whether such a thing as the soul exists at all, are questions entirely outside the scope of our respective conclusions.

The essential question may be put in these terms : Is the belief in immortality based on primitive error, or on some egotistical aspiration ; or, on the other hand, is it based on the partial recognition of truth ?

You, reader, if you desire a conclusion, must find your own. My intention has been to set before you a certain amount of suggestive material, without seeking to prejudice you unduly in the one direction or in the other. If your mind is already made up, I believe that you will have found in this book evidence which will confirm your opinion, whatever it may be. If, on the contrary, you are undecided, you will have found good reasons to justify your indecision. Listen, by way of epilogue, to the plaintive words of the Bushman, whose information on the subject of immortality is not less to be respected, I think, than yours or mine :

" The wind makes dust, because it means to blow away our footprints. And our gall, when we die, goes up among the stars : there it is, all green in the sky, when we are dead. When the moon stood hollow, mother was wont to speak in this fashion : mother said to us : ' Look ! the moon is carrying people who are dead : it lies all hollow because it is killing itself carrying people who are dead. Ye may hope to hear of something strange, when the moon lies in this manner.' And the hair of our heads will be like clouds when we die ; when we become as clouds."

BIBLIOGRAPHY

THIS list of books is necessarily incomplete. It includes most of the works consulted by the author, but periodicals and journals are omitted.

AMÉLINEAU, E.—Histoire de la Sépulture (Egypt). 1896.

AMYRAUT, M.—Estat des Fidèles après la Mort. 1646.

AYRTON, E. R., and W. S. LOAT.—The Predynastic Cemetery at El Mahasna. 1911.

BASDEN, G. T.—Among the Ibos of Nigeria. 1921.

BEECHAM, J.—Ashantee and the Gold Coast. 1841.

BIGELOW, W. S.—Buddhism and Immortality. 1908.

BLEEK, W. H., and L. LLOYD.—Specimens of Bushman Folklore. 1911.

BORLASE, W. C.—Naenia Cornubiae. 1872.

BOULE, M.—Les Hommes Fossiles. 1923.

BRITISH MUSEUM.—
Guide to the Bronze Age.
Guide to the Early Iron Age.
Guide to the Stone Age.

BROWN, A. R.—The Andaman Islanders. 1922.

BROWNE, SIR THOMAS.—Hydriotaphia. *Var. ed.*

BRUSTON, C. A.—Vie Future. 1890.

BUDGE, E. A. T. W.—
Book of Opening the Mouth. 1909.
Egyptian Heaven and Hell. 1906.
Liturgy of Funerary Offerings. 1909.
Osiris and the Egyptian Resurrection. 1911.

BUSHNELL, D. I.—Native Cemeteries (American Indians). 1920.

CHASSINAT, E.—Nécropole d'Assiout. 1911.

CHYTRAEUS, D.—De Morte et Vita Aeterna. 1583.

COBB, A. C.—Earth-burial and Cremation. 1892.

CODRINGTON, R. H.—The Melanesians. 1891.

DAVIES, N. DE G.—Five Theban Tombs. 1913.

DE MORGAN, J.—
    Les Premières Civilisations. 1909.
    Prehistoric Man (trs.). 1924.

DÉCHELETTE, J.—Manuel d'Archéologie Préhistorique, etc.
        1908, 1910, 1914.

FECHT, J.—De Statu Damnatorum. 1708.

FLAMMARION, C.—
    L'Inconnu. 1900.
    La Mort et son Mystère. 1920, 1922.

FOÀ, E.—Le Dahomey. 1895.

FOX, C. E.—The Threshold of the Pacific. 1925.

FRAZER, J. G.—
    Folklore of the Old Testament. 1918.
    The Belief in Immortality : Melanesians, Polynesians,
        Micronesians. 1913, 1922, 1924.
    The Golden Bough. Pt. 4. 1914.

GANN, T. W. F.—The Maya Indians of Yucatan, etc. 1919.

GARSTANG, J.—
    Burial Customs of Ancient Egypt. 1907.
    Tombs of the Third Dynasty at Reqaqnah. 1904.

GREENWELL, W.—British Barrows. 1877.

HOBLEY, C. W.—Bantu Beliefs and Magic. 1922.

HOSE, C., and W. MCDOUGALL.—The Pagan Tribes of
    Borneo. 1912.

HOWITT, A. W.—The Native Tribes of South-East Australia.
    1904.

KEYSERLING, H. VON.—Unsterblichkeit. 1920.

LE BRAZ, A.—La Légende de la Mort en Basse-Bretagne.
    1902.

LODGE, O. J.—The Survival of Man. 1909.

MACALISTER, R. A. S.—Text-Book of European Archaeology:
    Palaeolithic Period. 1921.

MACCULLOCH, J. A.—Religion of the Ancient Celts. 1911.

MAINAGE, T.—Religion de la Préhistoire. 1921.

MARIETTE, F. A. F.—Mastabas de L'Ancien Empire. 1889.

MASPERO, G.—Études. 5–8. 1911–1916.

MONTELIUS, O.—La Suède Préhistorique (Fr. trs.). 1874.

MOSSO, A.—The Dawn of Mediterranean Civilisation (trs.). 1910.

MURRAY, M. A.—Ancient Egyptian Legends. 1913.

MYERS, F. W. H.—
Human Personality. 1903.
Science and a Future Life. 1893.

PERUCCI, F.—Pompe Funebre di tutte le Nationi. 1639.

RASMUSSEN, K.—People of the Polar North (trs.). 1908.

RICHET, C.—Thirty Years of Psychic Research (trs.). 1923.

RIVERS, W. H. R.—
History of Melanesian Society. 1914.
The Todas. 1906.

ROSCOE, J.—
The Bagesu. 1924.
The Bakitara. 1923.

ROTH, H. L.—
Natives of Sarawak and British North Borneo. 1896.
The Aborigines of Tasmania. 1890, 1899.

SCHLIEMANN, H.—Mycenæ. 1878.

SCHWEINFURTH, G.—The Heart of Africa (trs.). 1874.

SELIGMANN, C. G. and B. Z.—The Veddas. 1911.

SKERTCHLY, J. A.—Dahomey as it is. 1874.

SMITH, G. E.—Migrations of Early Culture. 1915.

SPENCER, B.—Native Tribes of the Northern Territory (Australia). 1914.

SPENCER, B., and F. J. GILLEN.—Native Tribes of Central Australia. 1899.

TYLOR, E. B.—The Limits of Savage Religion. 1892.

UHLEMANN, M. A.—Todtengericht. 1854.

VULLIAMY, C. E.—Our Prehistoric Forerunners. 1925.

INDEX